EndNote 2/10/06

P9-AQM-570

EVALUATION TOOLKIT LIBRARY
ETS   Research Division
Princeton, New Jersey

CASE STUDY RESEARCH

Third Edition

Applied Social Research Methods Series
Volume 5

APPLIED SOCIAL RESEARCH
METHODS SERIES

Series Editors
LEONARD BICKMAN, Peabody College, Vanderbilt University, Nashville
DEBRA J. ROG, Vanderbilt University, Washington, DC

1. **SURVEY RESEARCH METHODS**
   (Third Edition)
   by FLOYD J. FOWLER, Jr.
2. **SYNTHESIZING RESEARCH**
   (Third Edition)
   by HARRIS COOPER
3. **METHODS FOR POLICY RESEARCH**
   by ANN MAJCHRZAK
4. **SECONDARY RESEARCH**
   (Second Edition)
   by DAVID W. STEWART
   and MICHAEL A. KAMINS
5. **CASE STUDY RESEARCH**
   (Third Edition)
   by ROBERT K. YIN
6. **META-ANALYTIC PROCEDURES FOR**
   SOCIAL RESEARCH
   (Revised Edition)
   by ROBERT ROSENTHAL
7. **TELEPHONE SURVEY METHODS**
   (Second Edition)
   by PAUL J. LAVRAKAS
8. **DIAGNOSING ORGANIZATIONS**
   (Second Edition)
   by MICHAEL I. HARRISON
9. **GROUP TECHNIQUES FOR**
   IDEA BUILDING (Second Edition)
   by CARL M. MOORE
10. **NEED ANALYSIS**
    by JACK McKILLIP
11. **LINKING AUDITING AND**
    META EVALUATION
    by THOMAS A. SCHWANDT
    and EDWARD S. HALPERN
12. **ETHICS AND VALUES**
    IN APPLIED SOCIAL RESEARCH
    by ALLAN J. KIMMEL
13. **ON TIME AND METHOD**
    by JANICE R. KELLY
    and JOSEPH E. McGRATH
14. **RESEARCH IN HEALTH CARE SETTINGS**
    by KATHLEEN E. GRADY
    and BARBARA STRUDLER WALLSTON
15. **PARTICIPANT OBSERVATION**
    by DANNY JORGENSEN
16. **INTERPRETIVE INTERACTIONISM**
    (Second Edition)
    by NORMAN K. DENZIN
17. **ETHNOGRAPHY**
    (Second Edition)
    by DAVID M. FETTERMAN
18. **STANDARDIZED SURVEY INTERVIEWING**
    by FLOYD J. FOWLER, Jr.
    and THOMAS W. MANGIONE
19. **PRODUCTIVITY MEASUREMENT**
    by ROBERT O. BRINKERHOFF
    and DENNIS E. DRESSLER
20. **FOCUS GROUPS**
    by DAVID W. STEWART
    and PREM N. SHAMDASANI
21. **PRACTICAL SAMPLING**
    by GART T. HENRY
22. **DECISION RESEARCH**
    by JOHN S. CARROLL
    and ERIC J. JOHNSON
23. **RESEARCH WITH HISPANIC**
    POPULATIONS
    by GERARDO MARIN
    and BARBARA VANOSS MARIN
24. **INTERNAL EVALUATION**
    by ARNOLD J. LOVE
25. **COMPUTER SIMULATION APPLICATIONS**
    by MARCIA LYNN WHICKER
    and LEE SIGELMAN
26. **SCALE DEVELOPMENT**
    by ROBERT F. DeVELLIS
27. **SUDYING FAMILIES**
    by ANNE P. COPELAND
    and KATHLEEN M. WHITE
28. **EVENT HISTORY ANALYSIS**
    by KAZUO YAMAGUCHI
29. **RESEARCH IN EDUCATIONAL SETTINGS**
    by GEOFFREY MARUYAMA
    and STANLEY DENO
30. **RESEARCHING PERSONS WITH**
    MENTAL ILLNESS
    by ROSALIND J. DWORKIN
31. **PLANNING ETHICALLY RESPONSIBLE**
    RESEARCH
    by JOAN E. SIEBER

Other volumes in this series are listed at the back of the book

CASE STUDY RESEARCH
Design and Methods

Third Edition

Robert K. Yin

Applied Social Research Methods Series
Volume 5

SAGE Publications
International Educational and Professional Publisher
Thousand Oaks ■ London ■ New Delhi

Copyright © 2003 by Sage Publications, Inc.

All rights reserved. No part of this book may be reproduced or utilized in any form or by any means, electronic or mechanical, including photocopying, recording, or by any information storage and retrieval system, without permission in writing from the publisher.

For information:

Sage Publications, Inc.
2455 Teller Road
Thousand Oaks, California 91320
E-mail: order@sagepub.com

Sage Publications Ltd.
6 Bonhill Street
London EC2A 4PU
United Kingdom

Sage Publications India Pvt. Ltd.
B-42 Panchsheel Enclave
Post Box 4109
New Delhi 110 017 India

Printed in the United States of America

Library of Congress Cataloging-in-Publication Data

Yin, Robert K.
Case study research : design and methods / Robert K. Yin.- 3rd ed.
    p. cm. — (Applied social research methods series ; v. 5)
Includes bibliographical references and index.
ISBN 0-7619-2552-X (alk. paper) - ISBN 0-7619-2553-8 (pbk. : alk. paper)
    1. CASE method. 2. Social sciences—Research—Methodology. I. Title.
II. Series.
H62 .Y56 2002
300′.7′22—dc21   2002152696

This book is printed on acid-free paper.

            04   05   06   10   9   8   7   6   5   4   3

Editorial Assistant:	Karen Wiley	
Production Editor:	Sanford Robinson	
Copy Editor:	Gillian Dickens	
Typesetter:	C&M Digitals (P) Ltd.	
Indexer:	Molly Hall	

Contents

Foreword	ix
Donald T. Campbell	
Preface	xiii
Additional Note About the Third Edition	xv

1. Introduction | 1
The Case Study as a Research Strategy | 1
Comparing Case Studies With Other Research
    Strategies in the Social Sciences | 3
Different Kinds of Case Studies, but a Common Definition | 11
Summary | 15

2. Designing Case Studies | 19
General Approach to Designing Case Studies | 19
Criteria for Judging the Quality of Research Designs | 33
Case Study Designs | 39
Modest Advice in Selecting Case Study Designs | 53

3. Conducting Case Studies: Preparing for Data Collection | 57
The Case Study Investigator: Desired Skills | 58
Training and Preparation for a Specific Case Study | 62
The Case Study Protocol | 67
Screening Case Study Nominations | 77
The Pilot Case Study | 78
Summary | 81

4. Conducting Case Studies: Collecting the Evidence | 83
Six Sources of Evidence | 85
Three Principles of Data Collection | 97
Summary | 106

5. Analyzing Case Study Evidence | 109
An Analytic Strategy: More Than
    Familiarity With Analytic Tools | 109
Specific Analytic Techniques | 116

    Pressing for a High-Quality Analysis   137
    Summary   138

6. Reporting Case Studies   141
    Targeting Case Study Reports   143
    Case Study Reports as Part of Larger, Multimethod Studies   150
    Illustrative Structures for Case Study Compositions   151
    Procedures in Doing a Case Study Report   155
    What Makes an Exemplary Case Study?   160

References   167

Index   175

About the Author   181

This book is dedicated to Hans-Lukas Teuber,
who made research a lifelong goal
for all who studied with him.

Foreword

It is a privilege to provide the foreword for this fine book. It epitomizes a research method for attempting valid inferences from events outside the laboratory while at the same time retaining the goals of knowledge shared with laboratory science.

More and more I have come to the conclusion that the core of the scientific method is not experimentation per se but rather the strategy connoted by the phrase "plausible rival hypotheses." This strategy may start its puzzle solving with evidence, or it may start with hypothesis. Rather than presenting this hypothesis or evidence in the context-independent manner of positivistic confirmation (or even of postpositivistic corroboration), it is presented instead in extended networks of implications that (although never complete) are nonetheless crucial to its scientific evaluation.

This strategy includes making explicit other implications of the hypothesis for other available data and reporting how these fit. It also includes seeking out rival explanations of the focal evidence and examining their plausibility. The plausibility of these rivals is usually reduced by ramification extinction, that is, by looking at their other implications on other data sets and seeing how well these fit. How far these two potentially endless tasks are carried depends on the scientific community of the time and what implications and plausible rival hypotheses have been made explicit. It is on such bases that successful scientific communities achieve effective consensus and cumulative achievements, without ever reaching foundational proof. Yet, these characteristics of the successful sciences were grossly neglected by the logical positivists and are underpracticed by the social sciences, quantitative or qualitative.

Such checking by other implications and the ramification-extinction of rival hypotheses also characterizes validity-seeking research in the humanities, including the hermeneutics of Schleiermacher, Dilthey, Hirst, Habermas, and current scholarship on the interpretation of ancient texts. Similarly, the strategy is as available for a historian's conjectures about a specific event as for a scientist's assertion of a causal law. It is tragic that major movements in the social sciences are using the term *hermeneutics* to connote giving up on the goal of validity and abandoning disputation as to who has got it right. Thus, in addition to the quantitative and quasi-experimental case study approach that Yin teaches, our social science methodological armamentarium also needs a humanistic validity-seeking case study methodology that, althoug making no use of quantification or tests of significance, would still work on the same questions and share the same goals of knowledge.

As versions of this plausible rival hypotheses strategy, there are two paradigms of the experimental method that social scientists may emulate. By training, we are apt to think first of the randomized-assignment-to-treatments model coming to us from agricultural experimentation stations, psychological laboratories, randomized trials of medical and pharmaceutical research, and the statistician's mathematical models. Randomization purports to control an infinite number of rival hypotheses *without specifying what any of them are.* Randomized assignment never completely controls these rivals but renders them implausible to a degree estimated by the statistical model.

The other and older paradigm comes from physical science laboratories and is epitomized by experimental isolation and laboratory control. Here are the insulated and lead-shielded walls; the controls for pressure, temperature, and moisture; the achievement of vacuums; and so on. This older tradition controls for a relatively few but explicitly specified rival hypotheses. These are never controlled perfectly, but well enough to render them implausible. Which rival hypotheses are controlled for is a function of the disputations current in the scientific community at the time. Later, in retrospect, it may be seen that other controls were needed.

The case study approach as presented here, and quasi-experimentation more generally, is more similar to the experimental isolation paradigm than to the randomized-assignment-to-treatments model in that each rival hypothesis must be specified and specifically controlled for. The degree of certainty or consensus that the scientific community is able to achieve will usually be less in out-of-doors social science, due to the lesser degree of plausibility-reduction of rival hypotheses that is likely to be achieved. The inability to replicate at will (and with variations designed to rule out specific rivals) is part of the problem. We should use those singular-event case studies (which can never be replicated) to their fullest, but we should also be alert for opportunities to do intentionally replicated case studies.

Given Robert Yin's background (Ph.D. in experimental psychology, with a dozen publications in that field), his insistence that the case study method be done in conformity with science's goals and methods is perhaps not surprising. But such training and career choice are usually accompanied by an intolerance of the ambiguities of nonlaboratory settings. I like to believe that this shift was facilitated by his laboratory research on that most hard-to-specify stimulus, the human face, and that this experience provided awareness of the crucial role of pattern and context in achieving knowledge.

This valuable background has not kept him from thoroughly immersing himself in the classic social science case studies and becoming in the process a leader of nonlaboratory social science methodology. I know of no comparable text. It meets a long-standing need. I am confident that it will become a standard text in social science research methods courses.

Donald T. Campbell
Bethlehem, Pennsylvania

Preface

The case study has long been (and continues to be) stereotyped as a weak sibling among social science methods. Investigators who do case studies are regarded as having downgraded their academic disciplines. Case studies have similarly been denigrated as having insufficient precision (i.e., quantification), objectivity, or rigor. This stereotype of case studies that began in the 20th century continues into the 21st century, especially compared to the computer-based advances in quantitative social science marked by computer-assisted telephone interview (CATI) techniques, clinical and community trial research designs, and analytic techniques such as structural equation modeling (SEMs) and hierarchical linear models (HLMs).

I wish I could paint a different picture. However, the stereotype does exist, and the warning is therefore quite simple: Do case studies, but do them with the understanding that your methods will be challenged from rational (and irrational) perspectives and that the insights resulting from your case studies may be underappreciated.

At the same time, derive comfort from the observation that, despite the stereotype of case studies as a weak method, case studies continue to be used extensively in social science research—including the traditional disciplines (psychology, sociology, political science, anthropology, history, and economics) as well as practice-oriented fields such as urban planning, public administration, public policy, management science, social work, and education. The method also is a frequent mode of thesis and dissertation research in all of these disciplines and fields. Moreover, case studies are increasingly commonplace even in evaluation research, supposedly the province of other methods such as surveys and quasi-experiments. All of this suggests a striking paradox: If the case study method has serious weaknesses, why do investigators continue to use it?

One possibility is that some people just do not know better and are not trained to use alternative methods. However, a perusal of the illustrative case studies cited as examples throughout this book will reveal a distinguished group of scholars, including a few who have served as heads of their respective professions (see the numbered BOXES throughout the text). A second, minor possibility is that U.S. federal agencies have made surveys and questionnaires a bureaucratically hazardous affair due to the clearance procedures required. Case studies therefore have become a preferred method. However, federally sponsored research does not dominate the social sciences—certainly not in Europe and other countries—and the nature of federal rules cannot account for the broader pattern of methodologies used in the social sciences. Furthermore, federal scrutiny in recent years also has enveloped the case study method.

In contrast, this book offers a third possibility—that the stereotype of the case study method may be wrong. According to this intriguing possibility, the continuing relevance of the method suggests that we have misunderstood its strengths and weaknesses; a different perspective may be needed. This book tries to develop such a perspective, by disentangling the case study as a research tool from (a) the case study as a teaching tool, (b) ethnographies and participant-observation, and (c) qualitative methods. The essence of the case study goes beyond all of these. Thus, the truly distinguishing features of the case study method, throughout all phases of research—problem definition, design, data collection, data analysis, and composition and reporting—are the topics of this book.

The object of the book is to guide investigators and students who are trying to do case studies as a rigorous method of research. The book claims to be distinctive in several ways. First, it is a comprehensive presentation of the case study method. Whereas other texts may cover only a few phases, this book can be (and apparently has been) used as a complete "cookbook" on case studies. Second, the book gives detailed attention to case study designs and analysis, compared to the traditional topic of case study data collection. The former have received too little attention in existing texts, yet they create the greatest problems for those doing case studies. Third, the book makes reference to case studies in many different fields, illustrating points made in the text (see the BOXES in the text). Finally, the book also is distinctive in that it is starting to pass the test of time, the first edition (1984) having gone through 8 printings, the revised edition (1989) through another 15, and the second edition (1994) yet another 14.

The ideas contained in this book stem from early case study methods courses taught at The Massachusetts Institute of Technology and at the American University, annual seminars under the auspices of the Aarhus School of Business in Denmark, and initial forays into the method during my career in policy research. However, the full evolution and maturation of these ideas have occurred through the numerous research projects conducted at COSMOS Corporation (from 1980 to the present), which have provided continuing opportunities if not demands for improving the craft and sharing it with others. Many of the cited applications of the case study method come from COSMOS's completed work (and many more will likely come from COSMOS's ongoing work).

In manuscript form, two anonymous reviewers commented helpfully on the first edition. Similarly, two anonymous reviewers provided detailed and extremely helpful comments on an early draft of this third edition. All four versions of this book (1984, 1989, 1994, and the present version) benefited directly from the continued and careful attention of Leonard Bickman and Debra Rog (the series editors), as well as of the fine editorial staff at Sage— Barbara Broka (1984 version), C. Deborah Laughton (1994 version), and copy editor Gillian Dickens (current version). Their attention, cheerful support, and periodic nudging all make an author want to finish a text. Nonetheless, as with the earlier versions, I alone bear the responsibility for this third edition.

Of course, anyone's ideas about case studies—and about social science methods more generally—must have deeper roots. Mine go back to the two disciplines in which I was trained: history as an undergraduate and experimental psychology as a graduate. History and historiography first raised my consciousness regarding the importance of methodology in the social sciences. The unique brand of basic research in experimental psychology I learned at MIT then taught me that empirical research advances only when it is accompanied by theory and logical inquiry and not when treated as a mechanistic or data collection endeavor. This lesson turns out to be a basic theme of the case study method. I have therefore dedicated this book to the person at MIT who taught me this best and under whom I completed a dissertation on face recognition, though he might only barely recognize the resemblances between past and present, were he alive today.

ADDITIONAL NOTE ABOUT THE THIRD EDITION

This third edition has been spruced up with numerous new examples of case study research (about 25% of the BOXES from the previous edition have been replaced, and the number of cited works also has been updated substantially) as well as new discussions about relevant developments in other methods—for example, randomized field trials (Chapter 1) and computer-assisted coding techniques (Chapter 5). In the updating process, one of the challenges has been to strike a balance between retaining citations from earlier years (for fear that they will be permanently lost to the new generation of scholars) and incorporating citations from recent years. The struggle resembles that between roots and relevance, and this third edition of the book hopefully maintains windows to both worlds.

More important than this updating, however, are expanded or new discussions on various facets of the case study method. In response to others' comments about the book, most of this expansion has occurred in Chapters 2 and 5, which apparently continue to provide well-appreciated guidance to case study investigators. In particular, Chapter 2 clarifies the strengths of multiple-case studies compared to single-case studies, especially the value of designing a "two-case" case study. Chapter 5 now presents fully five major analytic techniques, especially expanding on the use of logic models to guide analysis and also permitting the deletion of an earlier discussion of lesser modes of analysis. These and other examples, such as the discussion of case study screening (Chapter 3) and case studies as part of larger multi-method studies (Chapter 6), demonstrate that the case study craft not only can be updated but also can be upgraded. The upgrading produced a second challenge—avoiding the extremes of presenting a methodology that is either too basic or too obscure; The book should still provide practical and sound advice to be followed by novices and experienced investigators alike.

Yet a third general change has been the insertion of references (mostly in the notes at the end of each chapter) to examples of actual case studies that appear in the revised edition of a companion book, *Applications of Case Study Research* (2003). The companion book helps to meet yet another need expressed over the years—having access to case studies and not just advice about doing case studies. The references scattered throughout this book, to specific chapters in the companion book, tighten the relationship between principles for practice (this book) and samples from practice (the other book). Despite all these updates and changes, the text and chapters will appear largely similar to those of the second edition. The stability (not sterility!) is desirable because it reinforces the robustness of the basic case study method.

Throughout this entire process, I have carefully reviewed every word of the original text, still trying to improve sentence structure and syntax. Such editing is unending, compounded by the evolution of the American language—for example, "personal computers" instead of "microcomputers." Although the text is longer, I hope that it is easier to read.

I close this note by thanking all of you who have used this book over the past now-nearly 20 years. Comments about earlier versions suggest that the craft continues to advance, however haltingly. Understanding if not actual use of the method also appears more widespread. Whereas in 1984, the case study method appeared to be but a specialized niche in the repertoire of social science methods, figure and ground may have shifted. Most social scientists, whether wanting to practice case studies or not, now have some awareness and understanding of the method and may be increasingly using it in conjunction with other methods. These trends are heartening. Thank you all, once again.

1

Introduction

The case study is but one of several ways of doing social science research. Other ways include experiments, surveys, histories, and the analysis of archival information. Each strategy has peculiar advantages and disadvantages, depending on three conditions: (a) the type of research question, (b) the control an investigator has over actual behavioral events, and (c) the focus on contemporary as opposed to historical phenomena.

In general, case studies are the preferred strategy when "how" or "why" questions are being posed, when the investigator has little control over events, and when the focus is on a contemporary phenomenon within some real-life context. Such *explanatory* case studies also can be complemented by two other types—*exploratory* and *descriptive* case studies. Regardless of the type of case study, investigators must exercise great care in designing and doing case studies to overcome the traditional criticisms of the method.

THE CASE STUDY AS A RESEARCH STRATEGY

Using case studies for *research* purposes remains one of the most challenging of all social science endeavors. The purpose of this book is to help you—an experienced or budding social scientist—to deal with the challenge. Your goal is to design good case studies and to collect, present, and analyze data fairly. A further goal is to bring the case study to closure by writing a compelling report or book.

As a research strategy, the case study is used in many situations to contribute to our knowledge of individual, group, organizational, social, political, and related phenomena. Not surprisingly, the case study has been a common research strategy in psychology, sociology, political science, social work (Gilgun, 1994), business (Ghauri & Grønhaug, 2002), and community planning. Case studies are found even in economics, in which the structure of a given industry or the economy of a city or a region may be investigated by using the case study method. In all of these situations,

1

the distinctive need for case studies arises out of the desire to understand complex social phenomena. In brief, the case study method allows investigators to retain the holistic and meaningful characteristics of real-life events—such as individual life cycles, organizational and managerial processes, neighborhood change, international relations, and the maturation of industries.

This book covers the distinctive characteristics of the case study as a research method. The book will help you to deal with some of the more difficult questions still commonly neglected by available research texts. So often, for instance, the author has been confronted by a student or colleague who has asked (a) how to define the case being studied, (b) how to determine the relevant data to be collected, or (c) what should be done with the data, once collected. This book answers these questions and more by covering all of the phases of design, data collection, analysis, and reporting.

At the same time, the book does not cover all uses of case studies. For example, it is not intended to help those who might use case studies as teaching devices, popularized in the fields of law, business, medicine, or public policy (see Llewellyn, 1948; Stein, 1952; Towl, 1969; Windsor & Greanias, 1983) but now prevalent in virtually every academic field, including the natural sciences. For teaching purposes, a case study need not contain a complete or accurate rendition of actual events; rather, its purpose is to establish a framework for discussion and debate among students. The criteria for developing good cases for teaching—usually of the single- and not multiple-case variety—are far different from those for doing case study research (e.g., Caulley & Dowdy, 1987). Teaching case studies need not be concerned with the rigorous and fair presentation of empirical data; research case studies need to do exactly that.

Similarly, this book is not intended to cover those situations in which cases are used as a form of record keeping. Medical records, social work files, and other case records are used to facilitate some practice such as medicine, law, or social work. Again, the criteria for developing good cases for practice are different from those for designing case studies for research.

In contrast, the rationale for this book is that case studies have been increasingly used as a research tool (e.g., Hamel, 1992; Perry & Kraemer, 1986) and that you, as a social scientist, would like to know how to design and conduct single- or multiple-case studies to investigate a research issue. You may only be doing a case study or using it as part of a larger multimethod study (see Chapter 6). Whichever, this book concentrates heavily on the problem of designing and analyzing case studies. It is not merely a guide to collecting case study evidence. In this sense, the book fills a void in social science methodology, which has been dominated by texts on "fieldwork" and "field research" and, more recently, on "qualitative methods"—but that offer few guides on how to start a case study, analyze the data, or even minimize the problems of composing the case study report.

COMPARING CASE STUDIES WITH OTHER RESEARCH STRATEGIES IN THE SOCIAL SCIENCES

When and why would you want to do a case study on some topic? Should you consider doing an experiment instead? A survey? A history? A computer-based analysis of archival records, such as economic trends or student records?

These and other choices represent different research strategies. Each is a different way of collecting and analyzing empirical evidence, following its own logic. And each strategy has its own advantages and disadvantages. To get the most out of using the case study strategy, you need to appreciate these differences.[1]

A common misconception is that the various research strategies should be arrayed hierarchically. Many social scientists still deeply believe that case studies are only appropriate for the exploratory phase of an investigation, that surveys and histories are appropriate for the descriptive phase, and that experiments are the only way of doing explanatory or causal inquiries (e.g., Shavelson & Townes, 2002). This hierarchical view reinforces the idea that case studies are only a preliminary research strategy and cannot be used to describe or test propositions.

This hierarchical view, however, may be questioned. Experiments with an exploratory motive have certainly always existed. In addition, the development of causal explanations has long been a serious concern of historians, reflected by the subfield known as historiography. Likewise, case studies are far from being only an exploratory strategy. Some of the best and most famous case studies have been both explanatory case studies (e.g., see BOX 1 for a vignette on Allison and Zelikow's *Essence of Decision: Explaining the Cuban Missile Crisis*, 1999 [emphasis added]) and descriptive case studies (e.g., see BOX 2 for a vignette on Whyte's *Street Corner Society*, 1943/1955).[2]

The more appropriate view of these different strategies is an inclusive and pluralistic one. Each strategy can be used for all three purposes—exploratory, descriptive, or explanatory. There may be exploratory case studies, descriptive case studies, or explanatory case studies (Yin, 1981a, 1981b). There also may be exploratory experiments, descriptive experiments, and explanatory

---

BOX 1

A Best-Selling, Explanatory, Single-Case Study

For more than 30 years, Graham Allison's (1971) original study of a single case, the 1962 Cuban missile crisis—in which the U.S.–Soviet Union confrontation could have produced nuclear holocaust—has been a political science best-seller. The book posits three competing but also complementary theories to explain the crisis—that the United States and Soviet Union performed as (a) rationale actors, (b) complex bureaucracies, or (c) politically motivated groups of persons. Allison compares the ability of each one to explain the course of events in the crisis: why the Soviet Union placed offensive (and not merely defensive) missiles in Cuba in the first place, why the United States responded to the missile deployment with a blockade (and not an air strike or invasion—the missiles already were in Cuba!), and why the Soviet Union eventually withdrew the missiles.

The case study shows the explanatory and not just descriptive or exploratory functions of single-case studies. Furthermore, the lessons from the case study are intended to be generalizable not only to foreign affairs more broadly but also to a whole variety of complex governmental actions. In this way, the book, even more thoughtfully presented in its second edition (Allison & Zelikow, 1999), forcefully demonstrates how a single-case study can be the basis for significant explanations and generalizations.

BOX 2

A Famous Descriptive Case Study

Street Corner Society, by William F. Whyte (1943/1955), has for decades been recommended reading in community sociology. The book is a classic example of a descriptive case study. It traces the sequence of interpersonal events over time, describes a subculture that had rarely been the topic of previous study, and discovers key phenomena—such as the career advancement of lower-income youths and their ability (or inability) to break neighborhood ties.

The study has been highly regarded despite its being a single-case study, covering one neighborhood ("Cornerville") and a time period now more than 70 years old. The value of the book is, paradoxically, its generalizability to issues of individual performance, group structure, and the social structure of neighborhoods. Later investigators have repeatedly found remnants of Cornerville in their work, even though they have studied different neighborhoods and different time periods.

Strategy	Form of Research Question	Requires Control of Behavioral Events?	Focuses on Contemporary Events?
Experiment	how, why?	Yes	Yes
Survey	who, what, where, how many, how much?	No	Yes
Archival analysis	who, what, where, how many, how much?	No	Yes/No
History	how, why?	No	No
Case study	how, why?	No	Yes

Figure 1.1 Relevant Situations for Different Research Strategies
SOURCE: COSMOS Corporation.

experiments. What distinguishes the strategies is not this hierarchy but three other conditions, discussed below. Nevertheless, the clarification does not imply that the boundaries between the strategies—or the occasions when each is to be used—are always sharp. Even though each strategy has its distinctive characteristics, there are large overlaps among them. The goal is to avoid gross misfits—that is, when you are planning to use one type of strategy but another is really more advantageous.

When to Use Each Strategy

The three conditions consist of (a) the type of research question posed, (b) the extent of control an investigator has over actual behavioral events, and (c) the degree of focus on contemporary as opposed to historical events. Figure 1.1 displays these three conditions and shows how each is related to the five major research strategies being discussed: experiments, surveys, archival analyses, histories, and case studies. The importance of each condition, in distinguishing among the five strategies, is as follows.

Types of research questions (Figure 1.1, column 1). The first condition covers your research question(s) (Hedrick, Bickman, & Rog, 1993). A basic categorization scheme for the types of questions is the familiar series: "who," "what," "where," "how," and "why."

If research questions focus mainly on "what" questions, either of two possibilities arises. First, some types of "what" questions are exploratory, such as, "What can be learned from a study of an effective school?" This type of question is a justifiable rationale for conducting an exploratory study, the goal being to develop pertinent hypotheses and propositions for further inquiry. However, as an exploratory study, any of the five research strategies can be used—for example, an exploratory survey, an exploratory experiment, or an exploratory case study. The second type of "what" question is actually a form of a "how many" or "how much" line of inquiry—for example, "What have been the outcomes from a particular managerial restructuring?" Identifying such outcomes is more likely to favor survey or archival strategies than others. For example, a survey can be readily designed to enumerate the "what," whereas a case study would not be an advantageous strategy in this situation.

Similarly, like this second type of "what" question, "who" and "where" questions (or their derivatives—"how many" and "how much") are likely to favor survey strategies or the analysis of archival records, as in economic research. These strategies are advantageous when the research goal is to describe the incidence or prevalence of a phenomenon or when it is to be *predictive* about certain outcomes. The investigation of prevalent political attitudes (in which a survey or a poll might be the favored strategy) or of the spread of a disease like AIDS (in which an epidemiological analysis of health statistics might be the favored strategy) would be typical examples.

In contrast, "how" and "why" questions are more *explanatory* and likely to lead to the use of case studies, histories, and experiments as the preferred research strategies. This is because such questions deal with operational links needing to be traced over time, rather than mere frequencies or incidence. Thus, if you wanted to know how a community successfully overcame the negative impact of the closing of its largest employer—a military base (see Bradshaw, 1999)—you would be less likely to rely on a survey or an examination of archival records and might be better off doing a history or a case study. Similarly, if you wanted to know why bystanders fail to report emergencies under certain conditions, you could design and conduct a series of experiments (see Latané & Darley, 1969).

Let us take two more examples. If you were studying "who" had suffered as a result of terrorist acts and "how much" damage had been done, you might survey residents, examine business records (an archival analysis), or conduct a "windshield survey" of the affected area. In contrast, if you wanted to know "why" the act had occurred, you would have to draw on a wider array of documentary information, in addition to conducting interviews; if you focused on the "why" question in more than one terrorist act, you would probably be doing a multiple-case study.

Similarly, if you wanted to know "what" the outcomes of a new governmental program had been, you could answer this question by doing a survey or by examining economic data, depending on the type of program involved. Questions—for example, How many clients did the program serve? What kinds of benefits were received? How often were different benefits produced?—could all be answered without doing a case study. But if you needed to know "how" or "why" the program had worked (or not), you would lean toward either a case study or a field experiment.

To summarize, the first and most important condition for differentiating among the various research strategies is to identify the type of research question being asked. In general, "what" questions may either be exploratory (in which case any of the strategies could be used) or about prevalence (in which surveys or the analysis of archival records would be favored). "How" and "why" questions are likely to favor the use of case studies, experiments, or histories.

Defining the research questions is probably the most important step to be taken in a research study, so you should allow patience and sufficient time for this task. The key is to understand that research questions have both *substance* (e.g., What is my study about?) and *form* (e.g., Am I asking a "who," "what," "where," "why," or "how" question?). Others have focused on some of the substantively important issues (see Campbell, Daft, & Hulin, 1982); the point of the preceding discussion is that the form of the question can provide an important clue regarding the appropriate research strategy to be used. Remember, too, the large areas of overlap among the strategies, so that for some questions, a choice among strategies might actually exist. Be aware, finally, that you may be predisposed to pursue a particular strategy regardless of the study question. If so, be sure to create the form of the study question best matching the strategy you were inclined to pursue in the first place.

Extent of control over behavioral events (Figure 1.1, column 2) and degree of focus on contemporary as opposed to historical events (Figure 1.1, column 3). Assuming that "how" and "why" questions are to be the focus of study, a further distinction among history, case study, and experiment is the extent of the investigator's control over and access to actual behavioral events. Histories are the preferred strategy when there is virtually no access or control. The distinctive contribution of the historical method is in dealing with the "dead" past—that is, when no relevant persons are alive to report, even retrospectively, what occurred and when an investigator must rely on primary documents, secondary documents, and cultural and physical artifacts as the main sources of evidence. Histories can, of course, be done about contemporary events; in this situation, the strategy begins to overlap with that of the case study.

The case study is preferred in examining contemporary events, but when the relevant behaviors cannot be manipulated. The case study relies on many of the same techniques as a history, but it adds two sources of evidence not usually included in the historian's repertoire: direct observation of the events being studied and interviews of the persons involved in the events. Again, although case studies and histories can overlap, the case study's unique strength is its ability to deal with a full variety of evidence—documents, artifacts, interviews, and observations—beyond what might be available in a conventional historical study. Moreover, in some situations, such as participant-observation (see Chapter 4), informal manipulation can occur.

Finally, experiments are done when an investigator can manipulate behavior directly, precisely, and systematically. This can occur in a laboratory setting, in which an experiment may focus on one or two isolated variables (and presumes that the laboratory environment can "control" for all the remaining variables beyond the scope of interest), or it can be done in a field setting, where the term *social experiment* has emerged to cover research in which investigators "treat" whole groups of people in different ways, such as providing them with different kinds of vouchers (Boruch, 1993). Again, the methods overlap. The full range of experimental science also includes those situations in which the experimenter cannot manipulate behavior (see Blalock, 1961; Campbell & Stanley, 1966; Cook & Campbell, 1979) but in which the logic of experimental design may still be applied. These situations have been commonly regarded as "quasi-experimental" situations. The quasi-experimental approach can even be used in a historical setting, where, for instance, an investigator may be interested in studying race riots or lynchings (see Spilerman, 1971) and use a quasi-experimental design because no control over the behavioral event was possible.

In the field of evaluation research, Boruch and Foley (2000) have made a compelling argument for the practicality of one form of the quasi-experimental strategy—randomized field trials. The authors maintain that the field trials design can be and has been used even when evaluating complex community initiatives. If implementable, such a design is certainly superior to other designs because it produces greater certainty in the results. However, Boruch and Foley's pronouncements and review of the literature do not address common situations in which using randomized field trials is nevertheless difficult to implement if not totally infeasible. The situations include the following:

- the program being evaluated decides to fund specific sites on a competitive award procedure (the random field trials design requires random assignment to intervention and control groups);
- any comparison or control sites, selected to match the funded (intervention) sites, may already have in place or later adopt important components of the

funded intervention by using other resources (the design usually assumes that the intervention sites have the more potent intervention);

- the funded intervention may call for the community to reorganize its entire manner of providing certain services—that is, a "systems" change—thereby creating site-to-site variability in the unit of assignment or analysis (the design assumes that the unit of assignment is the same at every site, both intervention and control);

- the same systems change aspect of the intervention also may mean that the organizations or entities administering the intervention may not necessarily remain stable over the course of time (the design requires such stability until the random field trials have been completed);

- the funded intervention sites may be unwilling or unable to use the same instruments and measures (the design, which will ultimately "group" the data to compare intervention sites as a group with comparison sites as a second group, requires common instruments and measures across sites).

The existence of any of these conditions will likely lead to the need to find alternatives to randomized field trials.

Summary. You should be able to identify some situations in which all research strategies might be relevant (such as exploratory research) and other situations in which two strategies might be considered equally attractive. You also can use multiple strategies in any given study (e.g., a survey within a case study or a case study within a survey). To this extent, the various strategies are not mutually exclusive. But you should also be able to identify some situations in which a specific strategy has a distinct advantage. For the *case study*, this is when

- a "how" or "why" question is being asked about a contemporary set of events, over which the investigator has little or no control.

Determining the questions that are most significant for a topic and gaining some precision in formulating these questions requires much preparation. One way is to review the literature on the topic (Cooper, 1984). Note that such a literature review is therefore a means to an end and not—as many people have been taught to think—an end in itself. Novices may think that the purpose of a literature review is to determine the *answers* about what is known on a topic; in contrast, experienced investigators review previous research to develop sharper and more insightful *questions* about the topic.

Traditional Prejudices Against the Case Study Strategy

Although the case study is a distinctive form of empirical inquiry, many research investigators nevertheless disdain the strategy. In other words, as a research endeavor, case studies have been viewed as a less desirable form of inquiry than either experiments or surveys. Why is this?

Perhaps the greatest concern has been over the lack of rigor of case study research. Too many times, the case study investigator has been sloppy, has not followed systematic procedures, or has allowed equivocal evidence or biased views to influence the direction of the findings and conclusions. Such lack of rigor is less likely to be present when using the other strategies—possibly because of the existence of numerous methodological texts providing investigators with specific procedures to be followed. In contrast, few if any texts (besides the present one) cover the case study method in similar fashion.

The possibility also exists that people have confused case study teaching with case study research. In teaching, case study materials may be deliberately altered to demonstrate a particular point more effectively (e.g., Stein, 1952). In research, any such step would be strictly forbidden. Every case study investigator must work hard to report all evidence fairly, and this book will help her or him to do so. What is often forgotten is that bias also can enter into the conduct of experiments (see Rosenthal, 1966) and the use of other research strategies, such as designing questionnaires for surveys (Sudman & Bradburn, 1982) or conducting historical research (Gottschalk, 1968). The problems are not different, but in case study research, they may have been more frequently encountered and less frequently overcome.

A second common concern about case studies is that they provide little basis for scientific generalization. "How can you generalize from a single case?" is a frequently heard question. The answer is not simple (Kennedy, 1976). However, consider for the moment that the same question had been asked about an experiment: "How can you generalize from a single experiment?" In fact, scientific facts are rarely based on single experiments; they are usually based on a multiple set of experiments that have replicated the same phenomenon under different conditions. The same approach can be used with multiple-case studies but requires a different concept of the appropriate research designs, discussed in detail in Chapter 2. The short answer is that case studies, like experiments, are generalizable to theoretical propositions and not to populations or universes. In this sense, the case study, like the experiment, does not represent a "sample," and in doing a case study, your goal will be to expand and generalize theories (analytic generalization) and not to enumerate frequencies (statistical generalization). Or, as three notable social scientists describe in their *single* case study done years ago, the goal is to do a "generalizing" and not a "particularizing" analysis (Lipset, Trow, & Coleman, 1956, pp. 419-420).

A third frequent complaint about case studies is that they take too long and result in massive, unreadable documents. This complaint may be appropriate, given the way case studies have been done in the past (e.g., Feagin, Orum, & Sjoberg, 1991), but this is not necessarily the way case studies—yours included—must be done in the future. Chapter 6 discusses alternative ways of writing the case study—including ones in which the traditional, lengthy narrative can be avoided altogether. Nor need case studies take a long time. This incorrectly confuses the case study method with a specific method of data collection, such as ethnography (e.g., Fetterman, 1989) or participant-observation (e.g., Jorgensen, 1989). Ethnographies usually require long periods of time in the "field" and emphasize detailed, observational evidence. Participant-observation may not require the same length of time but still assumes a hefty investment of field efforts. In contrast, case studies are a form of inquiry that does *not* depend solely on ethnographic or participant-observer data. You could even do a valid and high-quality case study without leaving the library and the telephone or Internet, depending on the topic being studied.

Despite the fact that these common concerns can be allayed, as above, one major lesson is that good case studies are still difficult to do. The problem is that we have little way of screening or testing for an investigator's ability to do good case studies. People know when they cannot play music; they also know when they cannot do mathematics beyond a certain level; and they can be tested for other skills, such as the bar examination in law. Somehow, the skills for doing good case studies have not yet been defined, and as a result,

> most people feel that they can prepare a case study, and nearly all of us believe we can understand one. Since neither view is well founded, the case study receives a good deal of approbation it does not deserve. (Hoaglin, Light, McPeek, Mosteller, & Stoto, 1982, p. 134)

This quotation is from a book by five prominent *statisticians*. Surprisingly, even from another field, they recognize the challenge of doing good case studies.

DIFFERENT KINDS OF CASE STUDIES, BUT A COMMON DEFINITION

Our discussion has progressed without a formal definition of case studies. Moreover, commonly asked questions about case studies have still been unanswered. For example, is it still a case study when more than one case is included in the same study? Do case studies preclude the use of quantitative evidence? Can case studies be used to do evaluations? Let us now attempt to define the case study strategy and answer these questions.

Definition of the Case Study as a Research Strategy

The most frequently encountered definitions of case studies have merely repeated the types of topics to which case studies have been applied. For example, in the words of one observer,

> The essence of a case study, the central tendency among all types of case study, is that it tries to illuminate a *decision* or set of decisions: why they were taken, how they were implemented, and with what result. (Schramm, 1971, emphasis added)

This definition thus cites the topic of "decisions" as the major focus of case studies. Other topics have been similarly cited, including "individuals," "organizations," "processes," "programs," "neighborhoods," "institutions," and even "events."[3] However, citing the topic is surely insufficient to establish the needed definition of case studies.

Alternatively, most social science textbooks have failed to consider the case study a formal research method at all (the major exception is the book by five statisticians from Harvard University—Hoaglin et al., 1982). As discussed earlier, one common flaw was to consider the case study as the exploratory stage of some other type of research strategy, and the case study itself was only mentioned in a line or two of text.

Another definitional flaw has been to confuse case studies with ethnographies or with participant-observation, so that a textbook's presumed discussion of case studies was in reality a description either of the ethnographic method or of participant-observation as a data collection technique. Many standard methodological texts (e.g., see the earlier ones by Kidder & Judd, 1986; Nachmias & Nachmias, 1992), in fact, still cover "fieldwork" only as a data collection technique and omit any further discussion of case studies.

In a historical overview of the case study in American methodological thought, Jennifer Platt (1992a) explains the reasons for these treatments. She traces the practice of doing case studies back to the conduct of life histories, the work of the Chicago school of sociology, and casework in social work. She then shows how "participant-observation" emerged as a data collection technique, leaving the further definition of any distinctive case study method in suspension. Finally, she explains how the first edition of this book (1984) definitively dissociated the case study strategy from the limited perspective of doing participant-observation (or any type of field-work). The case study strategy, in her words, begins with "a logic of design . . . a strategy to be preferred when circumstances and research problems are appropriate rather than an ideological commitment to be followed whatever the circumstances" (Platt, 1992a, p. 46).

And just what is this logic of design? The technically critical features had been worked out prior to the first edition of this book (Yin, 1981a, 1981b) but now may be restated in two ways. First, the technical definition begins with the scope of a case study:

1. A case study is an empirical inquiry that

- investigates a contemporary phenomenon within its real-life context, especially when
- the boundaries between phenomenon and context are not clearly evident.

In other words, you would use the case study method because you deliberately wanted to cover contextual conditions—believing that they might be highly pertinent to your phenomenon of study. This first part of our logic of design therefore helps us to understand case studies by continuing to distinguish them from the other research strategies that have been discussed.

An experiment, for instance, deliberately divorces a phenomenon from its context, so that attention can be focused on only a few variables (typically, the context is "controlled" by the laboratory environment). A history, by comparison, does deal with the entangled situation between phenomenon and context, but usually with *non*contemporary events. Finally, surveys can try to deal with phenomenon and context, but their ability to investigate the context is extremely limited. The survey designer, for instance, constantly struggles to limit the number of variables to be analyzed (and hence the number of questions that can be asked) to fall safely within the number of respondents that can be surveyed.

Second, because phenomenon and context are not always distinguishable in real-life situations, a whole set of other technical characteristics, including data collection and data analysis strategies, now become the second part of our technical definition:

2. The case study inquiry

- copes with the technically distinctive situation in which there will be many more variables of interest than data points, and as one result

- relies on multiple sources of evidence, with data needing to converge in a triangulating fashion, and as another result
- benefits from the prior development of theoretical propositions to guide data collection and analysis.

In other words, the case study as a research strategy comprises an all-encompassing method—covering the logic of design, data collection techniques, and specific approaches to data analysis. In this sense, the case study is not either a data collection tactic or merely a design feature alone (Stoecker, 1991) but a comprehensive research strategy. How the strategy is defined and practiced is the topic of this entire book.

Certain other features of the case study strategy are not critical for defining the strategy but may be considered variations within case study research and also provide answers to common questions.

Variations Within Case Studies as a Research Strategy

Yes, case study research includes both single- and multiple-case studies. Though some fields, such as political science and public administration, have tried to distinguish sharply between these two approaches (and have used such terms as the *comparative case method* as a distinctive form of multiple-case studies) (see Agranoff & Radin, 1991; George, 1979; Lijphart, 1975), single- and multiple-case studies are in reality but two variants of case study designs (see Chapter 2 for more).

And, yes, case studies can include and even be limited to quantitative evidence. In fact, the contrast between quantitative and qualitative evidence does not distinguish the various research strategies. Note that, as analogous examples, some experiments (such as studies of psychophysical perceptions) and some survey questions (such as those seeking categorical rather than numerical responses) rely on qualitative and not quantitative evidence. Likewise, historical research can include enormous amounts of quantitative evidence.

As a related but important note, the case study strategy should not be confused with "qualitative research" (e.g., Denzin & Lincoln, 1994). Some qualitative research follows ethnographic methods and seeks to satisfy two conditions: (a) the use of close-up, detailed observation of the natural world by the investigator and (b) the attempt to avoid prior commitment to any theoretical model (Jacob, 1987, 1989; Lincoln & Guba, 1986; Stake, 1983; Van Maanen, Dabbs, & Faulkner, 1982, p. 16). However, ethnographic research does not always produce case studies (e.g., see the brief ethnographies in G. Jacobs, 1970), nor are case studies limited to these two conditions.

Instead, case studies can be based on any mix of quantitative and qualitative evidence. In addition, case studies need not always include direct, detailed observations as a source of evidence.

As a further note, some investigators distinguish between quantitative research and qualitative research—not on the basis of the type of evidence but on the basis of wholly different philosophical beliefs (e.g., Guba & Lincoln, 1989; Lincoln, 1991; Sechrest, 1991; Smith & Heshusius, 1986). These distinctions have produced a sharp debate within the field of evaluation research. Although some believe that these philosophical beliefs are irreconcilable, the counterargument can still be posed—that regardless of whether one favors qualitative or quantitative research, there is a strong and essential common ground between the two (Yin, 1994b).

And, yes, case studies have a distinctive place in evaluation research (see Cronbach et al., 1980; Guba & Lincoln, 1981; Patton, 1990; U.S. General Accounting Office, 1990). There are at least five different applications. The most important is to *explain* the presumed causal links in real-life interventions that are too complex for the survey or experimental strategies. In evaluation language, the explanations would link program implementation with program effects (U.S. General Accounting Office, 1990). A second application is to *describe* an intervention and the real-life context in which it occurred. Third, case studies can *illustrate* certain topics within an evaluation, again in a descriptive mode. Fourth, the case study strategy may be used to *explore* those situations in which the intervention being evaluated has no clear, single set of outcomes. Fifth, the case study may be a *meta-evaluation*—a study of an evaluation study (Smith, 1990; Stake, 1986). Whatever the application, one constant theme is that program sponsors— rather than research investigators alone—may have a prominent role in defining the evaluation questions and relevant data categories (U.S. General Accounting Office, 1990).

And finally, yes, case studies can be conducted and written with many different motives, including the simple presentation of individual cases or the desire to arrive at broad generalizations based on case study evidence (see BOX 3).

SUMMARY

This chapter has introduced the importance of the case study as a research method. The case study, like other research strategies, is a way of investigating an empirical topic by following a set of prespecified procedures. Articulating these procedures will dominate the remainder of this book.

BOX 3

Generalizing From Case Studies

Case study books can simply present individual case studies or also use the cases to make broader generalizations. Both approaches are found on a topic of continued public interest: identifying successful programs to improve U.S. social conditions.

3a. A Book That Does Not Generalize

Jonathan Crane (1998) edited a collection on nine programs, each presented in a separate chapter and written by a different author. The programs have in common strong evidence of their effectiveness, but they vary widely in their focus—from education to nutrition to drug prevention to preschool programs to drug treatment for delinquent youths. The aim of the book is to share this information, and the editor attempts no summary chapter, cross-program analysis, or generalizations.

3b. A Book That Does Generalize

Lisbeth Schorr's (1997) book is about major strategies for improving social conditions, illustrated by four policy topics: welfare reform, strengthening the child protection system, education reform, and transforming neighborhoods. The book is full of case studies of successful programs. Also citing data from the literature, the author develops numerous generalizations based on the case studies, including the need for successful programs to be "results oriented." Similarly, she identifies six other attributes of highly effective programs.

The chapter has provided an operational definition of the case study and has identified some of the variations in case studies. The chapter also has attempted to distinguish the case study from alternative research strategies in social science, indicating the situations in which doing a case study may be preferred, for instance, to doing a survey. Some situations may have no clearly preferred strategy, as the strengths and weaknesses of the various strategies may overlap. The basic goal, however, is to consider all the strategies in an inclusive and pluralistic fashion—as part of your repertoire from which you may draw according to a given situation to do social science research.

Finally, the chapter has discussed some of the major criticisms of case study research and has suggested that these criticisms are misdirected.

However, we must all work hard to overcome the problems of doing case study research, including the recognition that some of us were not meant, by skill or disposition, to do such research in the first place. Case study research is remarkably hard, even though case studies have traditionally been considered to be "soft" research, possibly because investigators have not followed systematic procedures. This book tries to make your research study easier by offering an array of such procedures.

EXERCISES

1. *Defining a case study question.* Develop a question that would be the rationale for a case study you might conduct. Instead of doing a case study, now imagine that you could only do a history, a survey, or an experiment (but not a case study) to answer this question. What aspects of the question, if any, could not be answered through these other research strategies? What would be the distinctive advantage of doing a case study in order to answer this question?

2. *Defining "significant" case study questions.* Name a topic you think is worthy of making the subject of a case study. Identify the three major questions your case study would try to answer. Now assume that you were actually able to answer these questions with sufficient evidence (i.e., that you had successfully conducted your case study). How would you justify, to a colleague, the significance of your findings? Would you have advanced some major theory? Would you have discovered something rare? (If you are unimpressed by your answers, perhaps you should consider redefining the major questions of your case.)

3. *Identifying "significant" questions in other research strategies.* Locate a research study based solely on the use of survey, historical, or experimental (but not case study) methods. Describe the ways in which the findings of this study are significant. Does it advance some major theory? Has it discovered something rare?

4. *Examining case studies used for teaching purposes.* Obtain a copy of a case study designed for teaching purposes (e.g., a case in a textbook used in a business school course). Identify the specific ways in which this type of "teaching" case is different from research case studies. Does the teaching case cite primary documents, contain evidence, or display data? Does the teaching case have a conclusion? What appears to be the main objective of the teaching case?

5. *Defining different types of case studies used for research purposes.* Define the three types of case studies used for research (but not teaching) purposes: (a) explanatory or causal case studies, (b) descriptive case studies, and (c) exploratory case studies. Compare the situations in which these different types of case studies would be most applicable, and then name a case study you would like to conduct. Would it be explanatory, descriptive, or exploratory? Why?

NOTES

1. The discussion only pertains to the use of these strategies in the social sciences, making no claims for commenting on the use of experiments, for instance, in physics, astronomy, or other fields.

2. Additional examples of explanatory case studies are presented in their entirety in a companion book, *Applications of Case Study Research* (Yin, 2003), in Chapters 4, 5, 6, and 7. Similarly, two examples of descriptive case studies are presented in their entirety in Chapters 2 and 3 of the same book.

3. Stake (1994) has a similar approach to defining case studies. He considers them not to be "a methodological choice but a choice of object to be studied." Furthermore, the object must be a "functioning specific" (such as a person or classroom) but not a generality (such as a policy).

2

Designing Case Studies

A research design is the logic that links the data to be collected (and the conclusions to be drawn) to the initial questions of study. Every empirical study has an implicit, if not explicit, research design. Articulating "theory" about what is being studied helps to operationalize case study designs and make them more explicit.

In addition, the development of case study designs needs to maximize four conditions related to design quality: (a) construct validity, (b) internal validity (for explanatory or causal case studies only), (c) external validity, and (d) reliability. How investigators deal with these aspects of quality control is summarized in Chapter 2 but also is a major theme throughout the remainder of the book.

Among the actual case study designs, four major types are relevant, following a 2 × 2 matrix. The first pair consists of single-case and multiple-case designs. The second pair, which can occur in combination with either of the first pair, is based on the unit or units of analysis to be covered—and distinguishes between holistic and embedded designs. Among these designs, most multiple-case designs are likely to be stronger than single-case designs. Trying to use even a "two-case" design is therefore a worthy objective compared to doing a single-case study.

GENERAL APPROACH TO DESIGNING CASE STUDIES

In identifying the research strategy for your research project, Chapter 1 has shown when you should select the case study strategy, as opposed to other strategies. The next task is to design your case study. For this purpose, as in designing any other type of research investigation, a plan, or *research design,* is needed.

The development of this research design is a difficult part of doing case studies. Unlike other research strategies, a comprehensive "catalog" of research designs for case studies has yet to be developed. There are no textbooks, like those in the biological and psychological sciences, covering such design considerations as the assignment of subjects to different "groups," the selection of different stimuli or experimental conditions, or the identification of various response measures (see Cochran & Cox, 1957; Fisher, 1935, cited in Cochran & Cox, 1957; Sidowski, 1966). In a laboratory experiment, each of these choices reflects an important logical connection to the issues being studied. Similarly, there are not even textbooks like the well-known volumes by Campbell and Stanley (1966) or by Cook and Campbell (1979) that summarize the various research designs for quasi-experimental situations. Nor have there emerged any common designs—for example, "panel" studies—such as those now recognized in doing survey research (see Kidder & Judd, 1986, chap. 6).

One pitfall to be avoided, however, is to consider case study designs to be a subset or variant of the research designs used for other strategies, such as experiments. For the longest time, scholars incorrectly thought that the case study was but one type of quasi-experimental design (the one-shot, posttest-only design). This misperception has finally been corrected, with the following statement appearing in a revision on quasi-experimental designs: "Certainly the case study as normally practiced should not be demeaned by identification with the one-group post-test-only design" (Cook & Campbell, 1979, p. 96). In other words, the one-shot, posttest-only design as a quasi-experimental design still may be considered flawed, but the case study has now been recognized as something different. In fact, the case study is a separate research method that has its own research designs.

Unfortunately, case study research designs have not been codified. The following chapter therefore expands on the new methodological ground broken by earlier editions of this book and describes a basic set of research designs for doing single- and multiple-case studies. Although these designs will need to be continually modified and improved in the future, in their present form, they will nevertheless help you to design more rigorous and methodologically sound case studies.

Definition of Research Designs

Every type of empirical research has an implicit, if not explicit, research design. In the most elementary sense, the design is the logical sequence that connects the empirical data to a study's initial research questions and, ultimately, to its conclusions. Colloquially, a research design is *a logical plan for getting from here to there,* where *here* may be defined as the initial set of questions to be answered, and *there* is some set of conclusions (answers) about these questions. Between "here" and "there" may be found a number of major steps, including the collection and analysis of relevant data. As a summary definition, another textbook has described a research design as a plan that

> guides the investigator in the process of collecting, analyzing, and interpreting observations. It is a *logical model of proof* that allows the researcher to draw inferences concerning causal relations among the variables under investigation. (Nachmias & Nachmias, 1992, pp. 77-78, emphasis added)

Another way of thinking about a research design is as a "blueprint" of research, dealing with at least four problems: what questions to study, what data are relevant, what data to collect, and how to analyze the results (Philliber, Schwab, & Samsloss, 1980).

Note that a research design is much more than a work plan. The main purpose of the design is to help to avoid the situation in which the evidence does not address the initial research questions. In this sense, a research design deals with a *logical* problem and not a *logistical* problem. As a simple example, suppose you want to study a single organization. Your research questions, however, have to do with the organization's relationships with other organizations—their competitive or collaborative nature, for example. Such questions can be answered only if you collect information directly from the other organizations and not merely from the one you started with. If you complete your study by examining only one organization, you cannot draw accurate conclusions about interorganizational partnerships. This is a flaw in your research design, not in your work plan. The outcome could have been avoided if you had developed an appropriate research design in the first place.

Components of Research Designs

For case studies, five components of a research design are especially important:

1. a study's questions;
2. its propositions, if any;
3. its unit(s) of analysis;
4. the logic linking the data to the propositions; and
5. the criteria for interpreting the findings.

Study questions. This first component has already been described in Chapter 1. Although the substance of your questions will vary, Chapter 1 suggested that the *form* of the question—in terms of "who," "what," "where," "how," and "why"—provides an important clue regarding the most relevant research strategy to be used. The case study strategy is most likely to be appropriate for "how" and "why" questions, so your initial task is to clarify precisely the nature of your study questions in this regard.

Study propositions. As for the second component, each proposition directs attention to something that should be examined within the scope of study. For instance, assume that your research, on the topic of interorganizational partnerships, began with the following question: How and why do organizations collaborate with one another to provide joint services (for example, a manufacturer and a retail store collaborating to sell certain computer products)? These "how" and "why" questions, capturing what you are really interested in answering, led you to the case study as the appropriate strategy in the first place. Nevertheless, these "how" and "why" questions do not point to what you should study.

Only if you are forced to state some propositions will you move in the right direction. For instance, you might think that organizations collaborate because they derive mutual benefits. This proposition, besides reflecting an important theoretical issue (that other incentives for collaboration do not exist or are unimportant), also begins to tell you where to look for relevant evidence (to define and ascertain the extent of specific benefits to each organization).

At the same time, some studies may have a legitimate reason for not having any propositions. This is the condition—which exists in experiments, surveys, and the other research strategies alike—in which a topic is the subject of "exploration." Every exploration, however, should still have some purpose. Instead of propositions, the design for an exploratory study should state this purpose, as well as the criteria by which an exploration will be judged successful. Consider the analogy in BOX 4 for exploratory case studies. Can you imagine how you would ask for support from Queen Isabella to do your exploratory study?

Unit of analysis. This third component is related to the fundamental problem of defining what the "case" is—a problem that has plagued many investigators at the outset of case studies. For instance, in the classic case study, a "case" may be an individual. Jennifer Platt (1992a, 1992b) has noted how the early case studies in the Chicago school of sociology were life histories of such roles as juvenile delinquents or derelict men. You also can imagine case studies of clinical patients, exemplary students, or political leaders. In each situation, an individual person is the case being studied, and the individual is the primary unit of analysis. Information about each

---

BOX 4

"Exploration" as an Analogy for an Exploratory Case Study

When Christopher Columbus went to Queen Isabella to ask for support for his "exploration" of the New World, he had to have some reasons for asking for three ships (Why not one? Why not five?), and he had to have some rationale for going westward (Why not south? Why not south and then east?). He also had some (mistaken) criteria for recognizing the Indies when he actually encountered it. In short, his exploration began with some rationale and direction, even if his initial assumptions might later have been proved wrong (Wilford, 1992). This same degree of rationale and direction should underlie even an exploratory case study.

---

relevant individual would be collected, and several such individuals or "cases" might be included in a multiple-case study. Propositions would still be needed to help identify the relevant information about this individual or individuals. Without such propositions, an investigator might be tempted to cover "everything," which is impossible to do. For example, the propositions in studying these individuals might involve the influence of early childhood or the role of peer relationships. Such topics already represent a vast narrowing of the relevant data. The more a study contains specific propositions, the more it will stay within feasible limits.

Of course, the "case" also can be some event or entity that is less well defined than a single individual. Case studies have been done about decisions, programs, the implementation process, and organizational change. Feagin et al. (1991) contains some classic examples of these single cases in sociology and political science. Beware of these types of topics—none is easily defined in terms of the beginning or end points of the "case." For example, a case study of a specific program may reveal (a) variations in program definition, depending on the perspective of different actors, and (b) program components that preexisted the formal designation of the program. Any case study of such a program would therefore have to confront these conditions in delineating the unit of analysis.

As a general guide, your tentative definition of the unit of analysis (and therefore of the case) is related to the way you have defined your initial research questions. Suppose, for example, you want to study the role of the United States in the world economy. Peter Drucker (1986) has written a provocative essay about fundamental changes in the world economy, including the importance of "capital movements" independent of the flow of goods and services. The unit of analysis for your case study might be a country's economy, an industry in the world marketplace, an economic policy, or the trade or capital flow between two countries. Each unit of analysis would call for a slightly different research design and data collection strategy.

Selection of the appropriate unit of analysis will occur when you accurately specify your primary research questions. If your questions do not lead to the favoring of one unit of analysis over another, your questions are probably either too vague or too numerous—and you may have trouble conducting your case study. However, when you have arrived at a definition of the unit of analysis, do not consider closure permanent. Your choice of the unit of analysis, as with other facets of your research design, can be revisited as a result of discoveries arising during your data collection (see discussion and cautions about flexibility, throughout and at the end of this chapter).

Sometimes, the unit of analysis may have been defined one way, even though the phenomenon being studied calls for a different definition. Most frequently, investigators have confused case studies of neighborhoods with case studies of small groups (as another example, confusing a new technology with the workings of an engineering team in an organization; see BOX 5A). How a geographic *area* such as a neighborhood copes with racial transition, upgrading, and other phenomena can be quite different from how a small *group* copes with these same phenomena. For instance, *Street Corner Society* (Whyte, 1943/1955—also see BOX 2 in Chapter 1 of this book) and *Tally's Corner* (Liebow, 1967—also see BOX 9, this chapter) have often been mistaken for being case studies of urban neighborhoods when in fact they are case studies of small groups (note that in neither book is the neighborhood geography described, even though the small groups lived in a small area with clear neighborhood implications). BOX 5B, however, presents a good example of how units of analyses can be defined in a more discriminating manner—in the field of world trade.

Most investigators will encounter this type of confusion in defining the unit of analysis. To reduce the confusion, one recommended practice is to discuss the potential case with a colleague. Try to explain to that person what questions you are trying to answer and why you have chosen a specific case or group of cases as a way of answering those questions. This may help you to avoid incorrectly identifying the unit of analysis.

Once the general definition of the case has been established, other clarifications in the unit of analysis become important. If the unit of analysis is a small group, for instance, the persons to be included within the group (the immediate topic of the case study) must be distinguished from those who are outside it (the context for the case study). Similarly, if the case is about

BOX 5A

What Is the Unit of Analysis?

The Soul of a New Machine was a Pulitzer Prize–winning book by Tracy Kidder (1981). The book, also a best-seller, is about the development of a new computer produced by Data General Corporation, intended to compete directly with one produced by Digital Equipment Corporation.

This easy-to-read book describes how Data General's engineering team invented and developed the new computer. The book begins with the initial conceptualization of the computer and ends when the engineering team relinquished control of the machine to Data General's marketing staff.

The book is an excellent example of a case study. However, the book also illustrates a fundamental problem in doing case studies—that of defining the *unit of analysis.* Is the case study about the computer, or is it about the dynamics of a small group—the engineering team? The answer is critical if we want to understand how the case study relates to a broader body of knowledge—that is, whether to generalize to a technology topic or to a group dynamics topic. Because the book is not an academic study, it does not need to, nor does it, provide an answer.

BOX 5B

A Clearer Choice Among Units of Analysis

Ira Magaziner and Mark Patinkin's (1989) book, *The Silent War: Inside the Global Business Battles Shaping America's Future,* presents nine case studies. Each case study helps the reader to understand a real-life situation of international economic competition.

Two of the cases appear similar but in fact have different main units of analysis. One case, about the Korean firm Samsung, is a case study of the critical policies that make the firm competitive. Understanding Korean economic development is part of the context, and the case study also contains an embedded unit—Samsung's development of the microwave oven as an illustrative product. The other case, about the development of an Apple computer factory in Singapore, is in fact a case study of Singapore's critical policies that make the country competitive. The Apple computer factory experience—an embedded unit of analysis—is actually an illustrative example of how the national policies affect foreign investments.

These two cases show how the definition of the main and embedded units of analyses, as well as the definition of the contextual events surrounding these units, depends on the level of inquiry. The main unit of analysis is likely to be at the level being addressed by the main study questions.

local services in a specific geographic area, decisions need to be made about those services whose district boundaries do not coincide with the area. Finally, for almost any topic that might be chosen, specific time boundaries are needed to define the beginning and end of the case. All of these types of questions need to be considered and answered to define the unit of analysis and thereby to determine the limits of the data collection and analysis.

One final point, pertaining to the role of the available research literature, needs to be made about defining the case and the unit of analysis. Most researchers will want to compare their findings with previous research; for this reason, key definitions used in your study should not be idiosyncratic. Rather, each case study and unit of analysis either should be similar to those previously studied by others or should innovate in clear, operationally defined ways. In this manner, the previous literature also can become a guide for defining the case and unit of analysis.

Linking data to propositions and criteria for interpreting the findings. The fourth and fifth components have been the least well developed in case studies. These components foreshadow the data analysis steps in case study research, and a research design should lay a solid foundation for this analysis.

Linking data to propositions can be done any number of ways, but none has become as precisely defined as the assignment of subjects and treatment conditions in psychological experiments (which is one way that hypotheses and data are connected in psychology). One promising approach for case studies is the idea of "pattern matching" described by Donald Campbell (1975), whereby several pieces of information from the same case may be related to some theoretical proposition (also see Chapter 5 of this book).

In a related article on one type of pattern—a time-series pattern—Campbell (1969) illustrates this approach. In the article, Campbell first showed how the annual number of traffic fatalities in Connecticut had seemed to decline after the passage of a new state law limiting the speed to 55 miles per hour. However, further examination of the fatality rate, over a number of years before and after the legal change, showed unsystematic fluctuation rather than any marked reduction. A simple eyeball test was all that was needed to show that the actual pattern *looked* unsystematic rather than following a downtrend (see Figure 2.1), and thus Campbell concluded that the speed limit had had no effect on the number of traffic fatalities.

What Campbell did was to describe two potential patterns and then show that the data matched one better than the other. If the two potential patterns are considered rival propositions (an "effects" proposition and a "no

a priori propositions:

Figure 2.1 An Example of Pattern Matching
SOURCE: COSMOS Corporation.

effects" proposition, regarding the impact of the new speed limit law), the pattern-matching technique is a way of relating the data to the propositions, even though the entire study consists of only a single case (the state of Connecticut).

This article also illustrates the problems in dealing with the fifth component, *the criteria for interpreting a study's findings.* Campbell's (1969) data matched one pattern better than they matched the other. But how close does a match have to be in order to be considered a match? Note that Campbell did not do any statistical test to make the comparison. Nor would a statistical test have been possible because each data point in the pattern was a single number—the number of fatalities for that year—for which one could not calculate a variance or conduct any statistical test. Currently, there is no precise way of setting the criteria for interpreting these types of findings. One hopes that the different patterns are sufficiently contrasting (as in Campbell's case) that the findings can be interpreted in terms of comparing at least two rival propositions. (Much more about the importance of such rivals appears in Chapter 5.)

Summary. A research design should include five components. Although the current state of the art does not provide detailed guidance on the last two, the complete research design should not only indicate what data are to be collected—as indicated by (a) a study's questions, (b) its propositions, and (c) its units of analysis. The design also should tell you what is to be done after the data have been collected—as indicated by (d) the logic linking the data to the propositions and (e) the criteria for interpreting the findings.

The Role of Theory in Design Work

Covering these preceding five components of research designs will effectively force you to begin constructing a preliminary theory related to your topic of study. This role of theory development, prior to the conduct of any data collection, is one point of difference between case studies and related methods such as ethnography (Lincoln & Guba, 1985, 1986; Van Maanen, 1988; Van Maanen et al., 1982) and "grounded theory" (Strauss & Corbin, 1998). Typically, these related methods deliberately avoid specifying any theoretical propositions at the outset of an inquiry. As a result, students confusing these methods with case studies wrongly think that by having selected the case study method, they can proceed quickly into the data collection phase of their work, and they may have been encouraged to make their "field contacts" as quickly as possible. No guidance could be more misleading. Among other considerations, the relevant field contacts depend on an understanding—or theory—of what is being studied.

Theory development. For case studies, theory development as part of the design phase is essential, whether the ensuing case study's purpose is to develop or test theory. Using a case study on the implementation of a new management information system (MIS) as an example (Markus, 1983), the simplest ingredient of a theory is a statement such as the following:

> The case study will show why implementation only succeeded when the organization was able to re-structure itself, and not just overlay the new MIS on the old organizational structure. (Markus, 1983)

The statement presents the nutshell of a theory of MIS implementation—that is, that organizational restructuring is needed to make MIS implementation work.

Using the same case, an additional ingredient might be the following statement:

The case study will also show why the simple replacement of key persons was not sufficient for successful implementation. (Markus, 1983)

This second statement presents the nutshell of a *rival* theory—that is, that MIS implementation fails because of the resistance to change on the part of individual people and that the replacement of such people is the only requirement for implementation to succeed.

You can see that as these two initial ingredients are elaborated, the stated ideas will increasingly cover the questions, propositions, units of analysis, logic connecting data to propositions, and criteria for interpreting the findings—that is, the five components of the needed research design. In this sense, the complete research design embodies a "theory" of what is being studied. This theory should by no means be considered with the formality of grand theory in social science, nor are you being asked to be a masterful theoretician. Rather, the simple goal is to have a sufficient blueprint for your study, and this requires theoretical propositions, usefully noted by two authors as "a [hypothetical] story about why acts, events, structure, and thoughts occur" (Sutton & Staw, 1995, p. 378). Then, the complete research design will provide surprisingly strong guidance in determining what data to collect and the strategies for analyzing the data. For this reason, theory development prior to the collection of any case study data is an essential step in doing case studies.

However, theory development takes time and can be difficult (Eisenhardt, 1989). For some topics, existing works may provide a rich theoretical framework for designing a specific case study. If you are interested in international economic development, for instance, Peter Drucker's (1986) "The Changed World Economy" is an exceptional source of theories and hypotheses. Drucker claims that the world economy had changed significantly from the past. He points to the "uncoupling" between the primary products (raw materials) economy and the industrial economy, a similar uncoupling between low labor costs and manufacturing production, and the uncoupling between financial markets and the real economy of goods and services. To test these propositions might require different studies, some focusing on the different uncouplings, others focusing on specific industries, and yet others explaining the plight of specific countries. Each different study would likely call for a different unit of analysis. Drucker's theoretical framework would provide guidance for designing these studies and even for collecting relevant data.

In other situations, the appropriate theory may be a descriptive theory (see BOX 6 and also BOX 2 earlier for another example), and your concern should focus on such issues as (a) the purpose of the descriptive effort,

---

BOX 6

Using a Metaphor to Develop Descriptive Theory

Whether four "countries"—the American colonies, Russia, England, and France—all underwent similar courses of events during their major political revolutions is the topic of Crane Brinton's (1938) famous historical study, *The Anatomy of a Revolution.* Tracing and analyzing these events is done in a descriptive manner, as the author's purpose is not so much to explain the revolutions as to determine whether they followed similar courses.

The "cross-case" analysis reveals major similarities: All societies were on the upgrade (not downgrade, as might have been expected) economically; there were bitter class antagonisms; the intellectuals deserted their governments; government machinery was inefficient; and the ruling class exhibited immoral, dissolute, or inept behavior (or all three). However, rather than relying solely on this "factors" approach to description, the author also develops the metaphor of a human body suffering from a fever as a way of describing the pattern of events over time. The author adeptly uses the cyclic pattern of fever and chills, rising to a critical point and followed by a false tranquility, to describe the ebb and flow of events in the four revolutions.

(b) the full but realistic range of topics that might be considered a "complete" description of what is to be studied, and (c) the likely topic(s) that will be the essence of the description. Good responses to these issues, including the rationales underlying the responses, will help you go a long way toward developing the needed theoretical base—and research design—for your study.

For yet other topics, the existing knowledge base may be poor, and the available literature will provide no conceptual framework or hypotheses of note. Such a knowledge base does not lend itself to the development of good theoretical statements, and any new empirical study is likely to assume the characteristic of an "exploratory" study. Nevertheless, as noted earlier with the illustrative case in BOX 4, even an exploratory case study should be preceded by statements about (a) what is to be explored, (b) the purpose of the exploration, and (c) the criteria by which the exploration will be judged successful.[1]

Illustrative types of theories. In general, to overcome the barriers to theory development, you should try to prepare for your case study by doing such things as reviewing the literature related to what you would like to study (also see Cooper, 1984), discussing your topic and ideas with colleagues or teachers, and asking yourself challenging questions about what you are studying, why you are proposing to do the study, and what you hope to learn as a result of the study.

As a further reminder, you should be aware of the full range of theories that might be relevant to your study. For instance, note that the MIS example illustrates MIS "implementation" theory, which is but one type of theory that can be the subject of study. Other types of theories for you to consider include the following:

- *Individual theories*—for example, theories of individual development, cognitive behavior, personality, learning and disability, individual perception, and interpersonal interactions
- *Group theories*—for example, theories of family functioning, informal groups, work teams, supervisory-employee relations, and interpersonal networks
- *Organizational theories*—for example, theories of bureaucracies, organizational structure and functions, excellence in organizational performance, and interorganizational partnerships
- *Societal theories*—for example, theories of urban development, international behavior, cultural institutions, technological development, and marketplace functions

Other examples cut across some of these illustrative types. Decision-making theory (Carroll & Johnson, 1992), for instance, can involve individuals, organizations, or social groups. As another example, a common topic of case studies is the evaluation of publicly supported programs, such as federal, state, or local programs. In this situation, the development of a theory of how a program is supposed to work is essential to the design of the evaluation but has been commonly underemphasized in the past (Bickman, 1987). According to Bickman (1987), analysts have frequently confused the theory of the program (e.g., how to make education more effective) with the theory of program implementation (e.g., how to install an effective program). Where policymakers want to know the desired substantive steps (e.g., describe a newly effective curriculum), the analysts unfortunately recommend managerial steps (e.g., hire a good project director). This mismatch can be avoided by giving closer attention to the substantive theory.

Generalizing from case study to theory. Theory development does not only facilitate the data collection phase of the ensuing case study. The appropriately developed theory also is the level at which the generalization of the case study results will occur. This role of theory has been characterized

Figure 2.2   Making Inferences: Two Levels
SOURCE: COSMOS Corporation.

throughout this book as "analytic generalization" and has been contrasted with another way of generalizing results, known as "statistical generalization." Understanding the distinction between these two types of generalization may be your most important challenge in doing case studies.

Let us first take the more commonly recognized way of generalizing— "statistical generalization"—although it is the less relevant one for doing case studies. In statistical generalization, an inference is made about a population (or universe) on the basis of empirical data collected about a sample. This is shown as a *Level One Inference* in Figure 2.2.[2] This method of generalizing is commonly recognized because research investigators have ready access to quantitative formulas for determining the confidence with which generalizations can be made, depending mostly on the size and internal variation within the universe and sample. Moreover, this is the most common way of generalizing when doing surveys (e.g., Fowler, 1988; Lavrakas, 1987) or analyzing archival data.

A fatal flaw in doing case studies is to conceive of statistical generalization as the method of generalizing the results of the case study. This is because your cases are not "sampling units" and should not be chosen for this reason. Rather, individual case studies are to be selected as a laboratory investigator selects the topic of a new experiment. Multiple cases, in this sense, should be considered like multiple experiments. Under these circumstances, the mode of generalization is "analytic generalization," in which a previously developed theory is used as a template with which to compare the empirical results of the case study. If two or more cases are shown to support the same theory, replication may be claimed. The empirical results may be considered yet more potent if two or more cases support the same theory but do not support an equally plausible, *rival* theory. Graphically, this type of generalization is shown as a *Level Two Inference* in Figure 2.2.

Analytic generalization can be used whether your case study involves one or several cases, which shall be later referenced as single-case or multiple-case studies. Furthermore, the logic of replication and the distinction between statistical and analytic generalization will be covered in greater detail in the discussion of multiple-case study designs. The main point at this juncture is that you should try to aim toward analytic generalization in doing case studies, and you should avoid thinking in such confusing terms as "the sample of cases" or the "small sample size of cases," as if a single case study were like a single respondent in a survey or a single subject in an experiment. In other words, in terms of Figure 2.2, you should aim for *Level Two Inferences* when doing case studies.

Because of the importance of this distinction between the two ways of generalizing, you will find repeated examples and discussion throughout the remainder of this chapter as well as in Chapter 5.

Summary. This subsection has suggested that a complete research design, covering the five components described earlier, in fact benefits from the development of a theoretical framework for the case study that is to be conducted. Rather than resisting such a requirement, a good case study investigator should make the effort to develop this theoretical framework, no matter whether the study is to be explanatory, descriptive, or exploratory. The use of theory, in doing case studies, is not only an immense aid in defining the appropriate research design and data collection but also becomes the main vehicle for generalizing the results of the case study.

CRITERIA FOR JUDGING
THE QUALITY OF RESEARCH DESIGNS

Because a research design is supposed to represent a logical set of statements, you also can judge the quality of any given design according to certain logical tests. Concepts that have been offered for these tests include trustworthiness, credibility, confirmability, and data dependability (U.S. General Accounting Office, 1990).

Four tests, however, have been commonly used to establish the quality of any empirical social research. Because case studies are one form of such

Tests	Case Study Tactic	Phase of research in which tactic occurs
Construct validity	● Use multiple sources of evidence	data collection
	● Establish chain of evidence	data collection
	● Have key informants review draft case study report	composition
Internal validity	● Do pattern-matching	data analysis
	● Do explanation-building	data analysis
	● Address rival explanations	data analysis
	● Use logic models	data analysis
External validity	● Use theory in single-case studies	research design
	● Use replication logic in multiple-case studies	research design
Reliability	● Use case study protocol	data collection
	● Develop case study database	data collection

Figure 2.3   Case Study Tactics for Four Design Tests
SOURCE: COSMOS Corporation.

research, the four tests also are relevant to case studies. An important innovation of this book is the identification of several tactics for dealing with these four tests when doing case studies. Figure 2.3 lists the four widely used tests and the recommended case study tactics, as well as a cross-reference to the phase of research when the tactic is to be used. (Each tactic is described in detail in the relevant chapter of this book.)

Because the four tests are common to all social science methods, the tests have been summarized in numerous textbooks (see Kidder & Judd, 1986, pp. 26-29):

- *Construct validity:* establishing correct operational measures for the concepts being studied
- *Internal validity* (for explanatory or causal studies only, and not for descriptive or exploratory studies): establishing a causal relationship, whereby certain conditions are shown to lead to other conditions, as distinguished from spurious relationships
- *External validity:* establishing the domain to which a study's findings can be generalized
- *Reliability:* demonstrating that the operations of a study—such as the data collection procedures—can be repeated, with the same results

This list is more complex than the standard "validity" and "reliability" concepts to which most students have been exposed, and each item deserves explicit attention. For case studies, an important revelation is that the several tactics to be used in dealing with these tests should be applied throughout the subsequent conduct of the case study and not just at the beginning. In this sense, "design work" actually continues beyond the initial design plans.

Construct Validity

This first test is especially problematic in case study research. People who have been critical of case studies often point to the fact that a case study investigator fails to develop a sufficiently operational set of measures and that "subjective" judgments are used to collect the data.[3] Take an example such as studying "neighborhood change"—a common case study topic (e.g., Bradshaw, 1999; Keating & Krumholz, 1999).

Over the years, concerns have arisen over how certain urban neighborhoods have changed their character. Any number of case studies have examined the types of changes and their consequences. However, without prior specification of the significant, operational events that constitute "change," a reader cannot tell whether the recorded changes in a case study genuinely reflect critical events in a neighborhood or whether they happen to be based on an investigator's impressions only.

Neighborhood change can indeed cover a wide variety of phenomena: racial turnover, housing deterioration and abandonment, changes in the pattern of urban services, shifts in a neighborhood's economic institutions, or the turnover from low- to middle-income residents in revitalizing neighborhoods. To meet the test of construct validity, an investigator must be sure to cover two steps:

1. Select the specific types of changes that are to be studied (and relate them to the original objectives of the study) and

2. Demonstrate that the selected measures of these changes do indeed reflect the specific types of change that have been selected.

For example, suppose you satisfy the first step by stating that you plan to study the rise in neighborhood crime. The second step now demands that you also justify why you might be using police-reported crime (which happens to be the standard measure used in the FBI Uniform Crime Reports) as your measure of crime. Perhaps this is not a valid measure, given that large proportions of crimes are not reported to the police.

As Figure 2.3 shows, three tactics are available to increase construct validity when doing case studies. The first is the use of *multiple sources of evidence,* in a manner encouraging convergent lines of inquiry, and this tactic is relevant during data collection (see Chapter 4). A second tactic is to establish a *chain of evidence,* also relevant during data collection (see also Chapter 4). The third tactic is to have the draft case study report reviewed by key informants (a procedure described further in Chapter 6).

Internal Validity

This second test has been given the greatest attention in experimental and quasi-experimental research (see Campbell & Stanley, 1966; Cook & Campbell, 1979). Numerous "threats" to validity have been identified, mainly dealing with spurious effects. However, because so many textbooks already cover this topic, only two points need to be made here.

First, internal validity is only a concern for causal (or explanatory) case studies, in which an investigator is trying to determine whether event x led to event y. If the investigator incorrectly concludes that there is a causal relationship between x and y without knowing that some third factor—z— may actually have caused y, the research design has failed to deal with some threat to internal validity. Note that this logic is inapplicable to descriptive or exploratory studies (whether the studies are case studies, surveys, or experiments), which are not concerned with making causal claims.

Second, the concern over internal validity, for case study research, may be extended to the broader problem of making inferences. Basically, a case study involves an inference every time an event cannot be directly observed. An investigator will "infer" that a particular event resulted from some earlier occurrence, based on interview and documentary evidence collected as part of the case study. Is the inference correct? Have all the rival explanations and possibilities been considered? Is the evidence convergent? Does it appear to be airtight? A research design that has anticipated these questions has begun to deal with the overall problem of making inferences and therefore the specific problem of internal validity.

However, the specific tactics for achieving this result are difficult to identify. This is especially true in doing case studies. As one set of suggestions, Figure 2.3 shows that the analytic tactic of *pattern matching,* already touched on but to be described further in Chapter 5, is one way of addressing internal validity. Three other analytic tactics—*explanation building, addressing rival explanations,* and *using logic models*—also are described in Chapter 5.

External Validity

The third test deals with the problem of knowing whether a study's findings are generalizable beyond the immediate case study. In the simplest example, if a study of neighborhood change focused on one neighborhood, are the results applicable to another neighborhood? The external validity problem has been a major barrier in doing case studies. Critics typically state that single cases offer a poor basis for generalizing. However, such critics are implicitly contrasting the situation to survey research, in which a sample (if selected correctly) readily generalizes to a larger universe. *This analogy to samples and universes is incorrect when dealing with case studies.* Survey research relies on *statistical* generalization, whereas case studies (as with experiments) rely on *analytical* generalization. In analytical generalization, the investigator is striving to generalize a particular set of results to some broader theory (see BOX 7).

For example, the theory of neighborhood change that led to a case study in the first place is the same theory that will help to identify the other cases to which the results are generalizable. If a study had focused on population transition in an urban neighborhood (e.g., Flippen, 2001), the procedure for selecting a neighborhood for study would have begun with identifying those types of neighborhoods within which transitions were occurring. Theories about population transition would then be the domain to which the results could later be generalized.

The generalization is not automatic, however. A theory must be tested by replicating the findings in a second or even a third neighborhood, where the theory has specified that the same results should occur. Once such direct replications have been made, the results might be accepted as providing strong support for the theory, even though further replications had not been performed. This *replication logic* is the same that underlies the use of experiments (and allows scientists to cumulate knowledge across experiments) and, as shown in Figure 2.3, will be discussed further in this chapter in the section on multiple-case designs.

Reliability

Most people are probably already familiar with this final test. The objective is to be sure that if a later investigator followed the same procedures as described by an earlier investigator and conducted the same case study all over again, the later investigator should arrive at the same findings and conclusions. (Note that the emphasis is on doing the *same* case over again, not on "replicating" the results of one case by doing another case study.) The goal of reliability is to minimize the errors and biases in a study.

BOX 7

How Case Studies Can Be Generalized to Theory

A common complaint about case studies is that it is difficult to generalize from one case to another. Thus, analysts fall into the trap of trying to select a "representative" case or set of cases. Yet no set of cases, no matter how large, is likely to deal satisfactorily with the complaint.

The problem lies in the very notion of generalizing to other case studies. Instead, an analyst should try to generalize findings to "theory," analogous to the way a scientist generalizes from experimental results to theory. (Note that the scientist does not attempt to select "representative" experiments.)

This approach is well illustrated by Jane Jacobs (1961) in her famous book, *The Death and Life of Great American Cities.* The book is based mostly on experiences from New York City. However, the chapter topics, rather than reflecting the single experiences of New York, cover broader theoretical issues in urban planning, such as the role of sidewalks, the role of neighborhood parks, the need for primary mixed uses, the need for small blocks, and the processes of slumming and unslumming. In the aggregate, these issues in fact represent the building of a theory of urban planning.

Jacobs's book created heated controversy in the planning profession. As a partial result, new empirical inquiries were made in other locales to examine one or another facet of her rich and provocative ideas. Her *theory,* in essence, became the vehicle for examining other cases, and the theory still stands as a significant contribution to the field of urban planning.

One prerequisite for allowing this other investigator to repeat an earlier case study is to document the procedures followed in the earlier case. Without such documentation, you could not even repeat your own work (which is another way of dealing with reliability). In the past, case study research procedures have been poorly documented, making external reviewers suspicious of the reliability of the case study.[4] As specific tactics to overcome these shortcomings, Chapter 3 discusses the use of a *case study protocol* to deal with the documentation problem in detail, and Chapter 4 describes another tactic, the development of a *case study database* (see Figure 2.3).

The general way of approaching the reliability problem is to make as many steps as operational as possible and to conduct research as if someone were always looking over your shoulder. In accounting and bookkeeping, one is always aware that any calculations must be capable of being audited. In this sense, an auditor is also performing a reliability check and must be able to produce the same results if the same procedures are followed. A good guideline for doing case studies is therefore to conduct the research so that an auditor could repeat the procedures and arrive at the same results.

Summary. Four tests may be considered relevant in judging the quality of a research design. In designing and doing case studies, various tactics are available to deal with these tests, though not all of the tactics occur at the formal stage of designing a case study. Some of the tactics occur during the data collection, data analysis, or compositional phases of the research and are therefore described in greater detail in subsequent chapters of this book.

CASE STUDY DESIGNS

These general characteristics of research designs serve as a background for considering the specific designs for case studies. Four types of designs will be discussed, based on a 2 × 2 matrix (see Figure 2.4). The matrix first shows that every type of design will include the desire to analyze contextual conditions in relation to the "case," and the dotted lines between the two indicate that the boundaries between the case and the context are not likely to be sharp. The matrix then shows that single- and multiple-case studies reflect different design situations and that within these two variants, there also can be a unitary unit or multiple units of analysis. The resulting four types of designs for case studies are single-case (holistic) designs (Type 1), single-case (embedded) designs (Type 2), multiple-case (holistic) designs (Type 3), and multiple-case (embedded) designs (Type 4). The rationale for these four types of designs is as follows.

What Are the Potential Single-Case Designs (Types 1 and 2)?

Rationale for single-case designs. A primary distinction in designing case studies is between *single-* and *multiple-*case designs. This means the need for a decision, prior to any data collection, on whether a single case study or multiple cases are going to be used to address the research questions. The single-case study is an appropriate design under several circumstances, and five rationales are given below. Recall that a single-case study is analogous to a single experiment, and many of the same conditions that justify a single experiment also justify a single-case study.

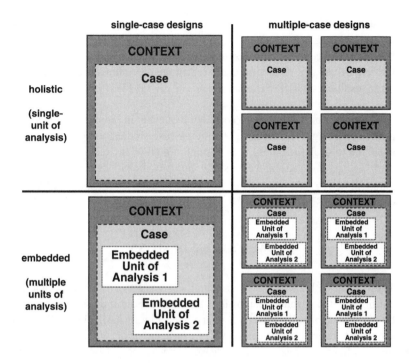

Figure 2.4   Basic Types of Designs for Case Studies
SOURCE: COSMOS Corporation.

One rationale for a single case is when it represents the *critical case* in testing a well-formulated theory (again, note the analogy to the critical *experiment*). The theory has specified a clear set of propositions as well as the circumstances within which the propositions are believed to be true. To confirm, challenge, or extend the theory, a single case may meet all of the conditions for testing the theory. The single case can then be used to determine whether a theory's propositions are correct or whether some alternative set of explanations might be more relevant. In this manner, like Graham Allison's (1971) comparison of three theories and the Cuban missile crisis (described in Chapter 1, BOX 1), the single case can represent a significant contribution to knowledge and theory building. Such a study can even help to refocus future investigations in an entire field. (See BOX 8 for another example, in the field of organizational innovation.)

A second rationale for a single case is when the case represents an *extreme* case or a *unique* case. Either of these situations commonly occurs

---

BOX 8

The Single Case Study as the Critical Case

One rationale for selecting a single-case rather than a multiple-case design is that the single case represents the *critical test of a significant theory*. Neal Gross et al. (1971) used such a design by focusing on a single school in their book, *Implementing Organizational Innovations*.

The school was selected because it had a prior history of innovation and could not be claimed to suffer from "barriers to innovation." In the prevailing theories, such barriers had been prominently cited as the major reason that innovations failed. Gross et al. showed that in this school, an innovation also failed but that the failure could not be attributed to any barriers. Implementation processes, rather than barriers, appeared to account for the outcomes.

In this manner, the book, though limited to a single case, represents a watershed in innovation theory. Prior to the study, analysts had focused on the identification of barriers; since the study, the literature has been much more dominated by studies of the implementation process.

---

in clinical psychology, in which a specific injury or disorder may be so rare that any single case is worth documenting and analyzing. For instance, one rare clinical syndrome is the inability of certain clinical patients to recognize familiar faces. Given visual cues alone, such patients are unable to recognize loved ones, friends, pictures of famous people, or (in some cases) their own image in a mirror. This syndrome appears to be due to some physical injury to the brain. Yet the syndrome occurs so rarely that scientists have been unable to establish any common patterns (Yin, 1970, 1978). In such circumstances, the single-case study is an appropriate research design whenever a new person with this syndrome—known as prosopagnosia—is encountered. The case study would document the person's abilities and disabilities, not only to determine the precise nature of the face recognition deficit but also to ascertain whether related disorders exist.

Conversely, a third rationale for a single case is the *representative* or *typical* case. Here, the objective is to capture the circumstances and conditions of an everyday or commonplace situation. The case study may represent a typical "project" among many different projects, a manufacturing firm believed to be typical of many other manufacturing firms in the same industry, a typical urban neighborhood, or a representative school, as examples. The lessons learned from these cases are assumed to be informative about the experiences of the average person or institution.

A fourth rationale for a single-case study is the *revelatory* case. This situation exists when an investigator has an opportunity to observe and analyze a phenomenon previously inaccessible to scientific investigation, such as Whyte's (1943/1955) *Street Corner Society*, previously described in Chapter 1, BOX 2. Another example is Elliot Liebow's (1967) famous case study of unemployed men, *Tally's Corner* (see BOX 9). Liebow had the opportunity to meet the men in one neighborhood in Washington, D.C., and to learn about their everyday lives. His observations of and insights into the problems of unemployment formed a significant case study because few social scientists had previously had the opportunity to investigate these problems, even though the problems were common across the country.(as distinguished from the rare or unique case). When other investigators have similar types of opportunities and can uncover some prevalent phenomenon previously inaccessible to scientists, such conditions justify the use of a single-case study on the grounds of its revelatory nature.

A fifth rationale for a single-case study is the *longitudinal* case: studying the same single case at two or more different points in time. The theory of interest would likely specify how certain conditions change over time, and the desired time intervals to be selected would reflect the presumed stages at which the changes should reveal themselves.

These five rationales serve as major reasons for conducting a single-case study. There are other situations in which the single-case study may be used as a pilot case that is the first of a multiple-case study. However, in these latter instances, the single-case study cannot be regarded as a complete study on its own.

Whatever the rationale for doing single cases (and there may be more than the five mentioned here), a potential vulnerability of the single-case design is that a case may later turn out not to be the case it was thought to be at the outset. Single-case designs therefore require careful investigation of the potential case to minimize the chances of misrepresentation and to maximize the access needed to collect the case study evidence. A fair warning is not to commit yourself to the single case until all of these major concerns have been covered.

Holistic versus embedded case studies. The same case study may involve *more than one unit of analysis.* This occurs when, within a single case, attention is also given to a subunit or subunits (see BOX 10). For instance, even though a case study might be about a single organization, such as a hospital, the analysis might include outcomes about the clinical services and staff employed by the hospital (and possibly even some quantitative analyses based on the employee records of the staff). In an evaluation

---

BOX 9

The Revelatory Case as a Single Case

Another rationale for selecting a single-case rather than a multiple-case design is that the investigator has access to a situation previously inaccessible to scientific observation. The case study is therefore worth conducting because the descriptive information alone will be revelatory.

Such was the situation in Elliot Liebow's (1967) sociological classic, *Tally's Corner.* The book is about a single group of men living in a poor, inner-city neighborhood. By befriending these men, the author was able to learn about their lifestyles, their coping behavior, and in particular their sensitivity to unemployment and failure. The book provided insights into a subculture that has prevailed in many U.S. cities for a long period of time, but one that had been only obscurely understood. The single case showed how investigations of such topics could be done, thus stimulating much further research and eventually the development of policy actions.

BOX 10

An Embedded, Single-Case Design

Union Democracy (1956) is a highly regarded case study by three eminent academicians—Seymour Martin Lipset, Martin Trow, and James Coleman. The case study is about the inside politics of the International Typographical Union and involves *several* units of analysis (see the following table). The main unit was the organization as a whole, the smallest unit was the individual member, and several intermediary units also were important. At each level of analysis, different data collection techniques were used, ranging from historical to survey analysis.

---

study, the single case might be a public program that involves large numbers of funded projects—which would then be the embedded units. In either situation, these embedded units can be selected through sampling or cluster techniques (McClintock, 1985). No matter how the units are selected, the resulting design would be called an *embedded case study design* (see Figure 2.4, Type 2). In contrast, if the case study examined only the global nature of an organization or of a program, a *holistic design* would have been used (see Figure 2.4, Type 1).

Kinds of Data (BOX 10 Continued)

Unit Being Characterized	Total System	Intermediate Units		Individuals	
	Issues, Data on Occupation; Union Laws; Policies; Historical Data; Convention Reports	*Locals' Histories and Voting Records; Issues on Local Level; Size of Locals*	*Shops' Voting Records; Shop Size*	*Interviews with Leaders*	*Interviews of the Sample of Man*
ITU as a whole	Structural, environmental, behavioral properties	By inference, communication network (structural)		Structural, environmental, behavioral properties	
Locals	Behavioral properties (militancy, etc.)	Behavioral properties, size	By inference, communication network (structural)		
Shops			Behavioral properties, size		Distributions of individual properties
Other immediate social environment of men	The social climate, by inference from dominant issues and election outcome	The social climate, by inference from dominant issues and election outcome			Chapel chairman's attributes; friends' attributes
Men	By inference, dominant values and interests	By inference: values, interests, and loyalties (e.g., local over international)	By inference: values, interests, loyalties (e.g., to shop over local)	By inference: values	Behavior, background, values, attitudes

SOURCE: Lipset, Trow, & Coleman (1956, p. 422). Reprinted by permission.

These two variants of single-case studies both have their strengths and weaknesses. The holistic design is advantageous when no logical subunits can be identified or when the relevant theory underlying the case study is itself of a holistic nature. Potential problems arise, however, when a global approach allows an investigator to avoid examining any specific phenomenon in operational detail. Thus, a typical problem with the holistic design is that the entire case study may be conducted at an abstract level, lacking any clear measures or data.

A further problem with the holistic design is that the entire nature of the case study may shift, unbeknownst to the researcher, during the course of study. The initial study questions may have reflected one orientation, but as the case study proceeds, a different orientation may emerge, and the evidence begins to address different research questions. Although some people have claimed such flexibility to be a strength of the case study approach, in fact, the largest criticism of case studies is based on this type of shift—in which the implemented research design is no longer appropriate for the research questions being asked (see COSMOS, 1983). Because of this problem, you need to avoid such unsuspected slippage; if the relevant research questions really do change, you should simply start over again, with a new research design. One way to increase the sensitivity to such slippage is to have a set of subunits. Thus, an embedded design can serve as an important device for focusing a case study inquiry.

An embedded design, however, also has its pitfalls. A major one occurs when the case study focuses only on the subunit level and fails to return to the larger unit of analysis. For instance, an evaluation of a program consisting of multiple projects may include project characteristics as a subunit of analysis. The project-level data may even be highly quantitative if there are many projects. However, the original evaluation becomes a project study (i.e., a multiple-case study of different projects) if no investigating is done at the level of the original case—that is, the program. Similarly, a study of organizational climate may involve individual employees as a subunit of study. However, if the data focus only on individual employees, the study will in fact become an employee and not an organizational study. In both examples, what has happened is that the original phenomenon of interest (a program or organizational climate) has become the context and not the target of study.

Summary. Single cases are a common design for doing case studies, and two variants have been described: those using holistic designs and those using embedded units of analysis. Overall, the single-case design is eminently justifiable under certain conditions—when the case represents (a) a critical test of existing theory, (b) a rare or unique circumstance, or (c) a representative or typical case or when the case serves a (d) revelatory or (e) longitudinal purpose.

A major step in designing and conducting a single case is defining the unit of analysis (or the case itself). An operational definition is needed and some precaution must be taken—before a total commitment to the whole case study is made—to ensure that the case in fact is relevant to the issues and questions of interest.

Within the single case may still be incorporated subunits of analyses, so that a more complex—or embedded—design is developed. The subunits can often add significant opportunities for extensive analysis, enhancing the insights into the single case. However, if too much attention is given to these subunits, and if the larger, holistic aspects of the case begin to be ignored, the case study itself will have shifted its orientation and changed its nature. If the shift is justifiable, you need to address it explicitly and indicate its relationship to the original inquiry.

What Are the Potential Multiple-Case Designs (Types 3 and 4)?

The same study may contain more than a single case. When this occurs, the study has used a multiple-case design, and such designs have increased in frequency in recent years. A common example is a study of school innovations (such as the use of new curricula, rearranged school schedules, or new educational technology), in which individual schools adopt some innovation. Each school is the subject of an individual case study, but the study as a whole covers several schools and in this way uses a multiple-case design.

Multiple- versus single-case designs. In some fields, multiple-case studies have been considered a different "methodology" from single-case studies. For example, both anthropology and political science have developed one set of rationales for doing single case studies and a second set for doing what have been considered "comparative" (or multiple-case) studies (see Eckstein, 1975; George, 1979; Lijphart, 1975). This book, however, considers single- and multiple-case designs to be variants within the same methodological framework—and no broad distinction is made between the so-called classic (i.e., single) case study and multiple-case studies. The choice is considered one of research design, with both being included under the case study method.

Multiple-case designs have distinct advantages and disadvantages in comparison to single-case designs. The evidence from multiple cases is often considered more compelling, and the overall study is therefore regarded as being more robust (Herriott & Firestone, 1983). At the same time, the rationale for single-case designs usually cannot be satisfied by multiple cases. The unusual or rare case, the critical case, and the revelatory case are all likely to involve only single cases, by definition. Moreover, the conduct of a multiple-case study can require extensive resources and time beyond the means of a single student or independent research investigator.

Therefore, the decision to undertake multiple-case studies cannot be taken lightly. Every case should serve a specific purpose within the overall scope of inquiry. Here, *a major insight is to consider multiple cases as one would consider multiple experiments*—that is, to follow a "replication" logic. This is far different from a mistaken analogy in the past, which incorrectly considered multiple cases to be similar to the multiple respondents in a survey (or to the multiple subjects within an experiment)—that is, followed a "sampling" logic. The methodological differences between these two views are revealed by the different rationales underlying the replication as opposed to sampling logics.

Replication, not sampling logic, for multiple-case studies. The replication logic is analogous to that used in multiple experiments (see Hersen & Barlow, 1976). For example, upon uncovering a significant finding from a single experiment, the immediate research goal would be to replicate this finding by conducting a second, third, and even more experiments. Some of the replications might have attempted to duplicate the exact conditions of the original experiment. Other replications might have altered one or two experimental conditions considered irrelevant to the original finding, to see whether the finding could still be duplicated. Only with such replications would the original finding be considered robust and worthy of continued investigation or interpretation.

The logic underlying the use of multiple-case studies is the same. Each case must be carefully selected so that it either (a) predicts similar results (a *literal replication*) or (b) predicts contrasting results but for predictable reasons (a *theoretical replication*). The ability to conduct 6 or 10 case studies, arranged effectively within a multiple-case design, is analogous to the ability to conduct 6 to 10 experiments on related topics; a few cases (2 or 3) would be literal replications, whereas a few other cases (4 to 6) might be designed to pursue two different patterns of theoretical replications. If all the cases turn out as predicted, these 6 to 10 cases, in the aggregate, would have provided compelling support for the initial set of propositions. If the cases are in some way contradictory, the initial propositions must be revised and retested with another set of cases. Again, this logic is similar to the way scientists deal with contradictory experimental findings.

An important step in all of these replication procedures is the development of a rich theoretical framework. The framework needs to state the conditions under which a particular phenomenon is likely to be found (a literal replication) as well as the conditions when it is not likely to be found (a theoretical replication). The theoretical framework later becomes the vehicle for generalizing to new cases, again similar to the role played in cross-experiment designs. Furthermore, just as with experimental science, if some of the empirical cases do not work as predicted, modification must be made to the theory. Remember, too, that theories can be practical and not just academic.

For example, one might consider the initial proposition that an increase in using computers in school districts will occur when such a technology is used for both administrative and instructional applications, but not either alone. To pursue this proposition in a multiple-case study design, 3 or 4 cases might be selected in which both types of applications are present, to determine whether, in fact, computer use did increase over a period of time (the investigation would be predicting a literal replication in these 3 or 4 cases). Three or 4 additional cases might be selected in which only administrative applications are present, with the prediction being little increase in use (predicting a theoretical replication). Finally, 3 or 4 other cases would be selected in which only instructional applications are present, with the same prediction of little increase in use, but for different reasons than the administrative-only cases (another theoretical replication). If this entire pattern of results across these multiple cases is indeed found, the 9 to 12 cases, in the aggregate, would provide substantial support for the initial proposition. BOX 11 summarizes another example of a multiple-case replication design, but from the field of urban studies.[5]

This replication logic, whether applied to experiments or to case studies, must be distinguished from the sampling logic commonly used in surveys. The sampling logic requires an operational enumeration of the entire universe or pool of potential respondents and then a statistical procedure for selecting a specific subset of respondents to be surveyed. The resulting data from the sample that is actually surveyed are assumed to reflect the entire universe or pool, with inferential statistics used to establish the confidence intervals for which this representation is actually accurate. The entire procedure is commonly used when an investigator wishes to determine the prevalence or frequency of a particular phenomenon.

Any application of this sampling logic to case studies would be misplaced. First, case studies are not the best method for assessing the prevalence of phenomena. Second, a case study would have to cover both the phenomenon of interest and its context, yielding a large number of potentially relevant variables. In turn, this would require an impossibly large number of cases—too large to allow any statistical consideration of the relevant variables.

BOX 11

A Multiple-Case Replication Design

A common problem of the 1960s and 1970s was how to get good advice to city governments. Peter Szanton's (1981) book, *Not Well Advised*, reviewed the experiences of numerous attempts by university and research groups to collaborate with city officials.

The study is an excellent example of a multiple-case replication design. Szanton starts with eight case studies, showing how different university groups all failed to help cities. The eight cases are sufficient "replications" to convince the reader of a general phenomenon. Szanton then provides five more case studies, in which nonuniversity groups also failed, concluding that failure was therefore not necessarily inherent in the academic enterprise. Yet a third group of cases shows how university groups have successfully helped business, engineering firms, and sectors other than city government. A final set of three cases shows that those few groups able to help city government were concerned with implementation and not just with the production of new ideas, leading to the major conclusion that city governments may have peculiar needs in receiving advice.

Within each of the four groups of case studies, Szanton has illustrated the principle of *literal* replication. Across the four groups, he has illustrated *theoretical* replication. This potent case study design can and should be applied to many other topics.

Third, if a sampling logic had to be applied to all types of research, many important topics could not be empirically investigated, such as the following problem: Your investigation deals with the role of the presidency of the United States, and you are interested in studying the behavior of the incumbent from some leadership perspective. The leadership perspective, to be at all faithful to the complexity of reality, must incorporate dozens if not hundreds of relevant variables. Any sampling logic simply would be misplaced under such circumstances, as there have been only 43 presidencies since the beginning of the Republic. Moreover, you would probably not have the resources to conduct a full study of all the presidencies (and even if you did, you would still have too many variables in relation to the 43 data points available). This type of study just could not be done, following the sampling logic; if the replication logic is followed, however, the study is eminently feasible.

The replication approach to multiple-case studies is illustrated in Figure 2.5. The figure indicates that the initial step in designing the study must consist of theory development and then shows that case selection and

Figure 2.5   Case Study Method
SOURCE: COSMOS Corporation.

the definition of specific measures are important steps in the design and data collection process. Each individual case study consists of a "whole" study, in which convergent evidence is sought regarding the facts and conclusions for the case; each case's conclusions are then considered to be the information needing replication by other individual cases. Both the individual cases and the multiple-case results can and should be the focus of a summary report. For each individual case, the report should indicate how and why a particular proposition was demonstrated (or not demonstrated). Across cases, the report should indicate the extent of the replication logic and why certain cases were predicted to have certain results, whereas other cases, if any, were predicted to have contrasting results.

An important part of Figure 2.5 is the dotted line feedback loop. The loop represents the situation in which important discovery occurs during the conduct of one of the individual case studies—for example, one of the cases did not in fact suit the original design. A second feedback loop (not shown) could represent the situation in which the discovery led to reconsidering one or more of the study's original theoretical propositions. Under either circumstance, "redesign" should take place before proceeding further. Such redesign might involve the selection of alternative cases or changes in the case study (i.e., data collection) protocol. Without such redesign, you risk being accused of distorting or ignoring the discovery, just to accommodate the original design. This condition leads quickly to a further accusation—that you have been selective in reporting your data to suit your preconceived ideas (i.e., the original theoretical propositions).

Overall, Figure 2.5 depicts a very different logic from that of a sampling design. The logic, as well as its contrast with a sampling design, may be difficult to follow and is worth extensive discussion with colleagues before proceeding with any case study design.

When using a multiple-case design, a further question you will encounter has to do with the *number* of cases deemed necessary or sufficient for your study. However, because a sampling logic should not be used, the typical criteria regarding sample size also are irrelevant. Instead, you should think of this decision as a reflection of the number of case replications—both literal and theoretical—that you need or would like to have in your study.

For the number of literal replications, an appropriate analogy from statistical studies is the selection of the criterion for establishing levels of significance: Much as the choice of "$p < .05$" or "$p < .01$" is not derived from any formula but is a matter of discretionary, judgmental choice, the selection of the number of replications depends on the certainty you want to have about your multiple-case results (as with the higher criterion for establishing statistical significance, the greater certainty lies with the larger number of cases). For example, you may want to settle for two or three literal replications when the rival theories are grossly different and the issue at hand does not demand an excessive degree of certainty. However, if your rivals have subtle differences or if you want a high degree of certainty, you may press for five, six, or more replications.

For the number of theoretical replications, the important consideration is related to your sense of the complexity of the realm of external validity. When you are uncertain whether external conditions will produce different case study results, you may want to articulate these relevant conditions more explicitly at the outset of your study and identify a larger number of cases to be included. For example, in studying neighborhood change, a common concern is that ethnically and racially different neighborhoods do not usually follow similar courses of change (e.g., Flippen, 2001). A multiple-case study of neighborhood change would therefore need to include at least some subgroups of cases that varied along ethnic or racial lines (and within each subgroup of cases, one would still want a minimum of two or three literal replications). In contrast, when external conditions are not thought to produce much variation in the phenomenon being studied, a smaller number of theoretical replications is needed.

Rationale for multiple-case designs. In short, the rationale for multiple-case designs derives directly from your understanding of literal and theoretical replications. The simplest multiple-case design would be the selection of two or more cases that are believed to be literal replications, such as a set of cases with exemplary outcomes in relation to some evaluation theory. Selecting such cases requires prior knowledge of the outcomes, with the multiple-case inquiry focusing on how and why the exemplary outcomes might have occurred and hoping for literal (or direct) replications of these conditions from case to case.

More complicated multiple-case designs would likely result from the number and types of theoretical replications you might want to cover. For example, investigators have used a "two-tail" design in which cases from both extremes (of some important theoretical condition, such as good and bad outcomes) have been deliberately chosen. Multiple-case rationales also can derive from the prior hypothesizing of different types of conditions and the desire to have subgroups of cases covering each type. These and other similar designs are more complicated because the study should still have at least two individual cases within each of the subgroups, so that the theoretical replications across subgroups are complemented by literal replications within each subgroup.

Multiple-case studies: Holistic or embedded. The fact that a design calls for multiple-case studies does not eliminate the variation identified earlier with single cases: Each individual case may still be holistic or embedded. In other words, a multiple-case study may consist of multiple holistic cases (see Figure 2.4, Type 3) or of multiple embedded cases (see Figure 2.4, Type 4).

The difference between these two variants depends on the type of phenomenon being studied and your research questions. In an embedded design, a study even may call for the conduct of a survey at each case study site. For instance, suppose a study is concerned with the delivery of services by different community mental health centers (Larsen, 1982). Each center may rightfully be the topic of a case study; the theoretical framework may dictate that nine such centers be included as case studies, three to replicate a direct result (literal replication) and six others to deal with contrasting conditions (theoretical replications).

For all nine centers, an embedded design is used because surveys of the centers' clients (or, alternatively, examination of clients' archival records) are needed to address research questions about the clients at the centers. However, the results of each survey will *not* be pooled across centers. Rather, the survey data will be part of the findings for each individual center, or case. These data may be highly quantitative, focusing on the attitudes and behavior of individual clients, and the data will be used along with archival information to interpret the success and operations at the given center. If, in contrast, the survey data are pooled across centers, a multiple-case study design is no longer being used, and the investigation is likely to be using a survey rather than case study design.

Summary. This section has dealt with situations in which the same investigation may call for multiple-case studies. These types of designs are becoming more prevalent, but they are more expensive and time-consuming to conduct.

Any use of multiple-case designs should follow a replication, not a sampling logic, and an investigator must choose each case carefully. The cases should serve in a manner similar to multiple experiments, with similar results (a literal replication) or contrasting results (a theoretical replication) predicted explicitly at the outset of the investigation.

The individual cases within a multiple-case study design may be either holistic or embedded. When an embedded design is used, each individual case study may in fact include the collection and analysis of highly quantitative data, including the use of surveys within each case.

MODEST ADVICE IN
SELECTING CASE STUDY DESIGNS

Now that you know how to define case study designs and are prepared to carry out design work, two pieces of advice may be offered.

Single- or Multiple-Case Designs?

The first word of advice is that although all designs can lead to successful case studies, when you have the choice (and resources), multiple-case designs may be preferred over single-case designs. Even if you can only do a "two-case" case study, your chances of doing a good case study will be better than using a single-case design. Single-case designs are vulnerable if only because you will have put "all your eggs in one basket." More important, the analytic benefits from having two (or more) cases may be substantial.

To begin with, even with two cases, you have the possibility of direct replication. Analytic conclusions independently arising from two cases, as with two experiments, will be more powerful than those coming from a single case (or single experiment) alone. Second, the contexts of the two cases are likely to differ to some extent. If under these varied circumstances you still can arrive at common conclusions from both cases, they will have immeasurably expanded the external generalizability of your findings, again compared to those from a single case alone.

BOX 12

Two "Two-Case" Case Studies

12a. Contrasting Cases for Community Building

Chaskin (2001) used two case studies to illustrate contrasting strategies for capacity building at the neighborhood level. The author's overall conceptual framework, which was the main topic of inquiry, claimed that there could be two approaches to building community capacity—using a collaborative organization to (a) reinforce existing networks of community organizations or (b) initiate a new organization in the neighborhood. After thoroughly airing the framework on theoretical grounds, the author presents the two case studies, showing the viability of each approach.

**12b. Contrasting Strategies
for Educational Accountability**

In a directly complementary manner, Elmore, Abelmann, and Fuhrman (1997) chose two case studies to illustrate contrasting strategies for designing and implementing educational accountability—that is, holding schools accountable for the academic performance of their students. One case represented a lower-cost, basic version of an accountability system. The other represented a higher-cost, more complex version.

Alternatively, you may have deliberately selected your two cases because they offered contrasting situations, and you were not seeking a direct replication. In this design, if the subsequent findings support the hypothesized contrast, the results represent a strong start toward theoretical replication—again vastly strengthening the external validity of your findings compared to those from a single case alone (e.g., see BOX 12).

In general, criticisms about single-case studies usually reflect fears about the uniqueness or artifactual condition surrounding the case (e.g., special access to a key informant). As a result, the criticisms may turn into skepticism about your ability to do empirical work beyond having done a single-case study. Having two cases can begin to blunt such criticism and skepticism. Having more than two cases will produce an even stronger effect. In the face of these benefits, having at least two cases should be your goal. If you do use a single-case design, you should be prepared to make an extremely strong argument in justifying your choice for the case.

Closed Designs or Flexible Designs?

Another word of advice is that despite this chapter's details about design choices, you should not think that a case study's design cannot be modified by new information or discovery during data collection. Such revelations can be enormously important, leading to your altering or modifying your original design.

As examples, in a single-case study, what was thought to be a critical or unique case might turn out not to be so after initial data collection has started; ditto a multiple-case study, in which what was thought to be parallel cases for literal replication turn out not to be so. Under these discoveries, you have every right to conclude that your initial design needs to be modified. However, you should undertake any alterations only given a serious caution. The caution is to understand precisely the nature of the alteration: Are you merely selecting different cases, or are you also changing your original theoretical concerns and objectives? The point is that the needed flexibility should not lessen the rigor with which case study procedures are followed.

EXERCISES

1. *Defining the boundaries of a case study.* Select a topic for a case study you would like to do. Identify some basic questions to be answered by your case study. Does the naming of these questions clarify the boundaries of your case, with regard to the relevant length of time for which evidence is to be collected? The relevant organization or geographic area? The type of evidence that should be collected? The priorities for doing analysis?

2. *Defining the unit of analysis for a case study.* Examine Figure 2.6. Discuss each topic, possibly citing an example of a published case study on each topic. Understanding that each topic illustrates a different unit of analysis, do you think the more concrete units are easier to define than the more abstract ones? Why?

3. *Defining the criteria for judging the quality of research designs.* Define the four criteria for judging the quality of research designs: (a) construct validity, (b) internal validity, (c) external validity, and (d) reliability. Give an example of each type of criterion in a case study you might want to do.

4. *Defining a case study research design.* Select one of the case studies described in the BOXES of this book. Describe the research design of this case study. How did it justify the relevant evidence to be sought, given the basic research questions to be answered? What methods were used to draw conclusions, based on the evidence? Is the design a single- or multiple-case design? Is it holistic, or does it have embedded units of analysis?

Figure 2.6   Illustrative Subjects of Case Studies
SOURCE: COSMOS Corporation.

5. *Establishing the rationale for single- and multiple-case studies.* Name the rationales for using a single-case study design and then name those for using a multiple-case design. Give examples of each type of design, either from the case studies described in the BOXES of this book or from other case studies with which you are acquainted. What are the advantages of each type of design?

NOTES

1. The companion book on *Applications of Case Study Research* (Yin, 2003) has a major chapter—see Chapter 1 of that book—on the role of theory in doing case studies, including extensive examples from four different case studies.

2. Figure 2.2 focuses only on the formal research design, not on data collection activities. For all three types of research, data collection techniques might be depicted as a third level—for example, for case studies, this might include using multiple sources of evidence, as described further in Chapter 4. Similar data collection techniques can be described for surveys or experiments—for example, questionnaire design for surveys or stimulus presentation strategies for experiments.

3. One of the anonymous reviewers of the draft version of this third edition points out that construct validity also has to do with whether interviewees understand what is being asked of them.

4. For other suggested guidelines for reviewers of case study proposals or manuscripts, see Yin (1999).

5. The companion book (Yin, 2003) contains three additional multiple-case studies, produced in their entirety in Chapters 8, 9, and 10, all designed to follow the replication logic.

3

Conducting Case Studies: Preparing for Data Collection

The preparation for doing a case study includes the prior skills of the investigator, the training and preparation for the specific case study, the development of a case study protocol, the screening of candidate case studies, and the conduct of a pilot case study. With regard to prior skills, many people incorrectly believe they are sufficiently skilled to do case studies because they think the method is easy to use. In fact, case study research is among the hardest types of research to do because of the absence of routine formulas.

To help prepare an investigator to do a high-quality case study, intensive training sessions should be planned. A case study protocol should be developed and refined. These procedures are especially desirable if the research is based on a multiple-case design, involves multiple investigators, or both.

Chapters 1 and 2 have shown that doing a case study begins with the definition of the problems or issues to be studied and the development of a case study design. However, most people associate the "doing" of a case study with the collection of the case study data, and this chapter and the following one focus on this activity. This chapter deals with preparing for data collection. The next covers the actual data collection techniques.

Preparing for data collection can be complex and difficult. If not done well, the entire case study investigation can be jeopardized, and all of the earlier work—in defining the research questions and designing the case study—will have been for naught.

Good preparation begins with *desired skills* on the part of the case study investigator. These skills have seldom been the subject of separate attention in the past. Yet some are critical and can be learned or practiced. Four additional topics also should be a formal part of any case study preparation: the *training* for a specific case study, the development of a *protocol* for the investigation, the *screening* of case study nominations, and the conduct of a *pilot case study.* The protocol is an especially effective way of dealing with the overall problem of increasing the reliability of case studies.

However, success with all five topics is needed to ensure that case study data collection will proceed smoothly. All demand a certain amount of patience, which has too frequently been overlooked in the past. The remainder of this chapter therefore discusses each topic.

THE CASE STUDY INVESTIGATOR:
DESIRED SKILLS

Too many people are drawn to the case study strategy because they believe it is "easy." Many social scientists—especially budding ones—think the case study strategy can be mastered without much difficulty. Their belief is that they will have to learn only a minimal set of technical procedures; that any of their own deficiencies in formal, analytic skills will be irrelevant; and that a case study will allow them simply to "tell it like it is." No belief could be farther from the truth.

In actuality, the demands of a case study on your intellect, ego, and emotions are far greater than those of any other research strategy. This is because the data collection procedures are *not* routinized. In laboratory experiments or in surveys, for instance, the data collection phase of a research project can be largely, if not wholly, conducted by one (or more) research assistant(s). The assistant is to carry out the data collection activities with a minimum of discretionary behavior, and in this sense, the activity is routinized—and analytically boring.

Conducting case studies offers no such parallel. Rather, a well-trained and experienced investigator is needed to conduct a high-quality case study because of the continuous interaction between the theoretical issues being studied and the data being collected. During data collection, only a more experienced investigator will be able to take advantage of unexpected opportunities rather than being trapped by them—and also will exercise sufficient care against potentially biased procedures.

Unfortunately, there are no tests for distinguishing those persons likely to become good case study investigators from those who are not. Compare this situation, briefly mentioned in Chapter 1, to that in mathematics or even a profession such as law. In math, people are able to score themselves for their abilities and to screen themselves from further advancement because they simply cannot carry out higher levels of math problems. To practice law, a person must first gain entrance into a law school and later pass the bar examination in a particular state. Again, many people screen themselves out of the field by failing to pass either of these tests.

No such gatekeepers exist for assessing case study skills. However, a basic list of commonly required skills is as follows:

- A good case study investigator should be able to *ask good questions*—and interpret the answers.
- An investigator should *be a good "listener"* and not be trapped by his or her own ideologies or preconceptions.
- An investigator should *be adaptive and flexible,* so that newly encountered situations can be seen as opportunities, not threats.
- An investigator must *have a firm grasp of the issues being studied,* whether this is a theoretical or policy orientation, even if in an exploratory mode. Such a grasp reduces the relevant events and information to be sought to manageable proportions.
- A person should *be unbiased by preconceived notions,* including those derived from theory. Thus, a person should be sensitive and responsive to contradictory evidence.

Each of these attributes is described below. Any absence of these attributes is remediable, and anyone missing one or more of the skills can work on developing them. But everyone must be honest in assessing her or his capabilities in the first place.

Question Asking

More than with the other research strategies discussed in Chapter 1, case studies require an inquiring mind *during* data collection, not just before or after the activity. The ability to pose and ask good questions is therefore a prerequisite for case study investigators. The desired result is for the investigator to create a rich dialogue with the evidence, an activity that encompasses

> pondering the possibilities gained from deep familiarity with some aspect of the world, systematizing those ideas in relation to kinds of information one might gather, checking the ideas in the light of that information, dealing with the inevitable discrepancies between what was expected and what was found by rethinking the possibilities of getting more data, and so on. (Becker, 1998, p. 66)

Case study data collection does follow a formal plan, but the specific information that may become relevant to a case study is not readily predictable. As you collect case study evidence, you must quickly review the evidence and continually ask yourself why events or facts appear as they do. Your judgments may lead to the immediate need to search for additional evidence.

If you are able to ask good questions throughout the data collection process, a good prediction is that you also will be mentally and emotionally exhausted at the end of each day. This depletion of analytic energy is far different from the experience in collecting experimental or survey data—that is, testing "subjects" or administering questionnaires. In these situations, data collection is highly routinized, and the data collector must complete a certain volume of work but exercise minimal discretionary behavior. Furthermore, any substantive review of the evidence does not come until some later time. The result is that such a data collector may become physically exhausted but will have been mentally untested after a day of data collection.

One insight into asking good questions is to understand that research is about questions and not necessarily about answers. If you are the type of person for whom one tentative answer immediately leads to a whole host of new questions, and if these questions eventually aggregate to some significant inquiry about how or why the world works as it does, you are likely to be a good asker of questions.

"Listening"

For case studies, "listening" means receiving information through multiple modalities—for example, making keen observations or sensing what might be going on—not just using the aural modality. Being a good "listener" means being able to assimilate large amounts of new information without bias. As an interviewee recounts an incident, a good listener hears the exact words used by the interviewee (sometimes, the terminology reflects an important orientation), captures the mood and affective components, and understands the context from which the interviewee is perceiving the world.

But the listening skill also needs to be applied to the inspection of documentary evidence, as well as to observations of real-life situations. In reviewing documents, listening takes the form of worrying whether there is any important message *between* the lines; any inferences, of course, would need to be corroborated with other sources of information, but important insights may be gained in this way. Poor "listeners" may not even realize that there can be information between the lines. Other listening deficiencies include having a closed mind or simply having a poor memory.

Adaptiveness and Flexibility

Very few case studies will end up exactly as planned. Inevitably, you will have to make minor if not major changes, ranging from the need to pursue an unexpected lead (potentially minor) to the need to identify a new "case" for study (potentially major). The skilled investigator must remember the original purpose of the investigation but then must be willing to adapt procedures or plans if unanticipated events occur (see BOX 13).

When a shift is made, you must maintain an unbiased perspective and acknowledge those situations in which, in fact, you may have inadvertently begun to pursue a totally new investigation. When this occurs, many completed steps—including the initial design of the case study—must be repeated and redocumented. One of the worst complaints about the conduct of case study research is that investigators change directions without knowing that their original research design was inadequate for the revised investigation, thereby leaving unknown gaps and biases. Thus, the need to balance adaptiveness with *rigor*—but not rigidity—cannot be overemphasized.

Grasp of the Issues Being Studied

The main way of staying on target, of course, is to understand the purpose of the case study investigation in the first place. Each case study investigator must understand the theoretical or policy issues because analytic judgments have to be made throughout the data collection phase. Without a firm grasp of the issues, you could miss important clues and would not know when a deviation was acceptable or even desirable. The point is that case study data collection is not merely a matter of *recording* data in a mechanical fashion, as it is in some other types of research. You also must be able to *interpret* the information as it is being collected and to know immediately, for instance, if several sources of information contradict one another and lead to the need for additional evidence—much like a good detective.

In fact, the detective role offers some rich insights into case study fieldwork. Note that the detective arrives on a scene *after* a crime has occurred and is basically being called on to make *inferences* about what actually transpired. The inferences, in turn, must be based on convergent evidence from witnesses and physical evidence, as well as some unspecifiable element of common sense. Finally, the detective may have to make inferences about multiple crimes, to determine whether the same perpetrator committed them. This last step is similar to the replication logic underlying multiple-case studies.

Lack of Bias

All of the preceding conditions will be negated if an investigator seeks to use a case study only to substantiate a preconceived position. Case study investigators are especially prone to this problem because they must

---

BOX 13

Maintaining Flexibility in Designing a Case Study

Peter Blau's (1955) study of behavior in large government agencies (*The Dynamics of Bureaucracy*) is still valued for its insights into the relationship between the formal and informal organization of work groups, even 50 years later.

Although his study focused on two government agencies, that was not Blau's initial design. As the author notes, he first intended to study a single organization and later switched to a plan to compare two organizations—a public one and a private one (pp. 272-273). However, his initial attempts to gain access to a private firm were unsuccessful, and meanwhile, he had developed a stronger rationale for comparing two government agencies, but of different kinds.

These shifts in the initial plans are examples of the kinds of changes that can occur in the design of a case study. Blau's experience shows how a skilled investigator can take advantage of changing opportunities, as well as shifts in theoretical concerns, to produce a classic case study.

---

understand the issues beforehand (see Becker, 1958, 1967). In contrast, the traditional research assistant, though mechanistic and possibly even sloppy, is not likely to introduce bias into the research.

One test of this possible bias is the degree to which you are open to contrary findings. For example, researchers studying "nonprofit" organizations may be surprised to find that many of these organizations have entrepreneurial and capitalistic motives. If such findings are based on compelling evidence, the conclusions of the case study would have to reflect these contrary findings. To test your own tolerance for contrary findings, report your preliminary findings—possibly while still in the data collection phase—to two or three critical colleagues. The colleagues should offer alternative explanations and suggestions for data collection. If the quest for contrary findings can produce documentable rebuttals, the likelihood of bias will have been reduced.

TRAINING AND PREPARATION
FOR A SPECIFIC CASE STUDY

The key to understanding the training needed for collecting case study data is to understand that every case study investigator must be able to operate as a "senior" investigator. Once you have started collecting data, you should think of yourself as an independent investigator who cannot rely on a rigid formula to guide your inquiry. You must be able to make intelligent decisions about the data being collected.

In this sense, training for a case study investigation actually begins with the definition of the questions being addressed and the development of the case study design. If these steps have been satisfactorily conducted, as described in Chapters 1 and 2, only minimal further effort may be needed, especially if there is only a single case study investigator.

However, it often happens that a case study investigation must rely on *multiple investigators,*[1] for any of three reasons:

1. a single case calls for intensive data collection at the same site, requiring a "team" of investigators (see BOX 14);
2. a case study involves multiple cases, with different persons being needed to cover each site or to rotate among the sites; or
3. a combination of the first two conditions.

Furthermore, some members of the research team may not have participated in the initial question-defining or research design phases of a study. Under these conditions, formal training and preparation are essential preludes to actual data collection.

Case Study Training as a Seminar Experience

When multiple investigators are to be trained, they all can learn to be "senior" investigators if the training takes the form of a seminar rather than rote instruction. As in a seminar, much time has to be allowed for reading, preparing for the training sessions, and the sessions themselves. In most instances, the seminar requires at least a week's worth of preparation and discussions. (See Figure 3.1 for an agenda of an illustrative training session.)

Typically, the seminar will cover all phases of the planned case study investigation, including readings on the subject matter, the theoretical issues that led to the case study design, and case study methods and tactics. The goal of the training is to have all participants understand the basic concepts, terminology, and issues relevant to the study. Each investigator needs to know:

- Why the study is being done
- What evidence is being sought
- What variations can be anticipated (and what should be done if such variations occur)
- What would constitute supportive or contrary evidence for any given proposition

---

BOX 14

The Logistics of Field Research, Circa 1924-1925

Arranging schedules and gaining access to relevant sources of evidence are important to the *management* of a case study. The modern researcher may feel that these activities have only emerged with the growth of "big" social science during the 1960s and 1970s.

In a famous field study done nearly a century ago, however, many of the same management techniques had already been practiced. The two principal investigators and their staff secretary opened a local office in the city they were studying. This office was used by other project staff for extended periods of time. From this vantage point, the research team participated in local life, examined documentary materials, compiled local statistics, conducted interviews, and distributed and collected questionnaires. This extensive fieldwork resulted 5 years later in the publication of the now-classic study of small-town America, *Middletown* (1929), by Robert and Helen Lynd.

Discussions, rather than lectures, are the key part of the training effort to ensure that the desired level of understanding has been achieved.

This seminar approach to case study training again can be contrasted to the training for other types of data collection—for example, group training for survey interviewers. The survey training does involve discussions, but it mainly emphasizes the questionnaire items or terminology to be used and takes place over an intensive but short period of time. Moreover, the training avoids the global or conceptual concerns of the study, as the interviewer is discouraged from having any broader understanding than the mechanics of the survey instrument. Survey training rarely involves any outside reading about the substantive issues, and the survey interviewer generally has no knowledge of how the survey data are to be analyzed or what issues are to be investigated. The ideal survey interviewer sticks closely to the prescribed set of questions in the survey instrument. Such an approach would be insufficient for case study training.

Protocol Development and Review

The next subsection will say more about the *content* of the case study protocol. However, a legitimate and desirable training task is the coauthorship of the protocol by all of the case study investigators.

I. Purpose of case studies and research questions (*hold a substantive discussion*)

II. Review of case study nominations and of nomination procedures (*review protocol used for screening the nominations*)

III. Schedule for doing case studies (*define deadlines*)

    A. Preparation period

    B. Arrangement of site visit (sample confirmation letter to site)

    C. Conduct of site visit

    D. Follow-up activities (sample thank-you letter)

    E. Preparation of case study report

    F. Submission of draft report to site, for review (sample transmittal letter)

IV. Review of case study protocol

    A. Discussion of relevant theoretical frameworks and literature

    B. Development or review of hypothetical logic model, if relevant (sample)

    C. In-depth discussion of protocol topics (*discuss importance of topic and possible types of evidence to be collected in relation to each topic*)

V. Outline of case study report (*have a draft outline, showing the major potential headings for the report*)

VI. Methodological reminders

    A. Fieldwork procedures (*discuss methodological principles*)

    B. Use of evidence (*review types of evidence and need for convergence*)

    C. Note taking and other field practices

    D. Other orienting topics

VII. Reading materials

    A. Sample case study reports (*refer to samples from related studies; review desirable and undesirable features of these samples*)

    B. Key substantive books and articles (*make sure the relative priorities among these works are appreciated*)

Figure 3.1 Training Session Agenda

A major task of the training seminar may therefore be to develop a draft protocol. In this situation, each investigator may be assigned one portion of the substantive topics to be covered by the case study. Each investigator is then responsible for reviewing the appropriate reading materials on the assigned portion, adding any other information that may be relevant, and drafting the initial set of protocol questions for that portion. In the seminar, the entire group of case study investigators can discuss and review the individual drafts. Such a discussion not only will lead to the completion of the protocol but also will ensure that each investigator has mastered the content of the protocol by having participated in its development.

If the case study team does not share the task of developing the protocol, the training sessions should include a thorough review of the protocol. All aspects of the protocol, whether procedural or substantive, need to be discussed, and modifications in the protocol may be made.

Problems to Be Addressed

The training also has the purpose of uncovering problems within the case study plan or the research team's capabilities. If such problems do emerge, one consolation is that they will be more troublesome if they are not recognized until later, after the data collection begins. Good case study investigators should therefore press to be certain, during the training period, that potential problems are brought into the open.

The most obvious problem is that the training may reveal flaws in the case study design or even the initial definition of the study questions. If this occurs, you must be willing to make the necessary revisions, even if more time and effort are necessary. Sometimes, the revisions will challenge the basic purpose of the investigation, as in a situation in which the original objective may have been to investigate a technological phenomenon, such as the use of personal computers, but in which the case study really turns out to be about an organizational phenomenon. Any revisions, of course, also may lead to the need to review a slightly different literature and to recast the entire study and its audience. Nevertheless, such changes are warranted if the training has demonstrated the unrealistic (or uninteresting) nature of the original plan.

A second problem is that the training sessions may reveal incompatibilities among the investigating team—particularly the fact that some of the investigators may not share the ideology of the project or its sponsors. In one multiple-case study of community organizations, for instance, the case study investigators varied in their beliefs regarding the efficacy of such organizations (U.S. National Commission on Neighborhoods, 1979). When such biases are discovered, one way of dealing with the contrary ideologies is to suggest to the investigators that contrary evidence will be respected if it is collected and verifiable. The investigator still has the choice, of course, of continuing to participate in the study or deciding to drop out.

A third problem is that the training may uncover some unreal time deadlines or expectations regarding available resources. For instance, a case study may have assumed that 20 persons were to be interviewed, in an open-ended manner, as part of the data collection. The training may have revealed, however, that the time needed for interviewing these persons is likely to be much longer than anticipated. Under such circumstances, any expectation that 20 persons could be interviewed would have to depend on revising the original data collection schedule.

Finally, the training may uncover some positive features, such as the fact that two or more investigators are able to work productively together. Such rapport and productivity during the training session may readily extend to the actual data collection period and may therefore suggest certain pairings for the case study teams. In general, the training should have the effect of creating group norms for the ensuing data collection activity. This norm-building process is more than an amenity; it will help ensure supportive reactions should unexpected problems arise during the data collection.

THE CASE STUDY PROTOCOL

A case study protocol has only one thing in common with a survey questionnaire: Both are directed at a single data point—collecting data either from a single-case study (even if the case study is part of a larger, multiple-case study) or from a single respondent.

Beyond this similarity are major differences. The protocol is more than a questionnaire or instrument. First, the protocol contains the instrument as well as the procedures and general rules to be followed in using the protocol. Second, the protocol is directed at an entirely different party than that of an instrument, explained below. Third, having a case study protocol is desirable under all circumstances, but it is essential if you are doing a multiple-case study.

The protocol is a major way of increasing the *reliability* of case study research and is intended to guide the investigator in carrying out the data collection from a single-case study (again, even if the single case is one of several in a multiple-case study). Figure 3.2 gives a table of contents from an illustrative protocol, which was used in a study of innovative law enforcement

A. Introduction to the case study and purpose of protocol

    A1 Case study questions, hypotheses, and propositions

    A2 Theoretical framework for the case study (*reproduces the logic model*)

    A3 Role of protocol in guiding the case study investigator (*notes that the protocol is a standardized agenda for the investigator's line of inquiry*)

B. Data collection procedures

    B1 Names of sites to be visited, including contact persons

    B2 Data collection plan (*covers the calendar period for the site visits, the amount of time to be used for each visit, and the level of effort to do each case study*)

    B3 Expected preparation prior to site visits (*identifies specific documents to be reviewed and where they can be accessed*)

C. Outline of case study report

    C1 The practice in operation

    C2 Innovativeness of the practice

    C3 Outcomes from the practice, to date

    C4 Law enforcement agency context and history pertaining to the practice

    C5 Attachments: chronology, specific logic model for the practice, references to relevant documents, and list of persons interviewed

D. Case study questions

    D1 The practice in operation and its innovativeness:

        a. Describe the practice in detail and the nature and amount of federal funding.

        b. What is the nature, if any, of collaborative efforts across communities or jurisdictions that has been needed to put the practice into place?

        c. How did the idea for the practice start?

        d. Was there a planning process, and how did it work? What were the original goals and target populations or areas for the practice?

        e. In what ways is the practice innovative, compared to other practices of the same kind or in the same jurisdiction?

        f. Describe how the practice is to continue after federal funding has ended.

    D2 Evaluation

        a. What is the design for evaluating the practice, and who is doing the evaluation?

        b. What part of the evaluation has been implemented?

        c. What are the outcome measures being used, and what outcomes have been identified to date?

        d. What rival explanations have been identified and explored for attributing the outcomes to the investment of the federal funds?

Figure 3.2   Table of Contents of a Protocol for Conducting Case Studies of Innovative Law Enforcement Practices

practices supported by federal funds. The practices had been defined earlier through a careful screening process (see a later discussion in this chapter for more detail on "screening case study nominations"). Furthermore, because data were to be collected from 18 such cases as part of a multiple-case study, the information about any given case could not be collected in great depth, and thus the number of the case study questions was minimal.

As a general matter, a case study protocol should have the following sections:

- An overview of the case study project (project objectives and auspices, case study issues, and relevant readings about the topic being investigated)
- Field procedures (presentation of credentials, access to the case study "sites," general sources of information, and procedural reminders)
- Case study questions (the specific questions that the case study investigator must keep in mind in collecting data, "table shells" for specific arrays of data, and the potential sources of information for answering each question—see Figure 3.3 for an example)
- A guide for the case study report (outline, format for the data, use and presentation of other documentation, and bibliographical information)

A quick glance at these topics will indicate why the protocol is so important. First, it keeps you targeted on the subject of the case study. Second, preparing the protocol forces you to anticipate several problems, including the way that the case study reports are to be completed. This means, for instance, that you will have to identify the *audience* for your case study report even before you have conducted your case study. Such forethought will help to avoid disastrous outcomes in the long run.

The table of contents of the illustrative protocol in Figure 3.2 reveals another important feature of the case study report: The outline starts by calling for a description of the innovative practice being studied (see item C1 in Figure 3.2)—and only later covers the agency context and history pertaining to the practice (see item C4). This choice reflects the fact that most investigators place too much emphasis (and write too extensively) on history and background conditions. Although these are important, the description of the subject of the study—in this situation, the innovative practice—needs more attention.

Each section of the protocol is discussed next.

Overview of the Case Study Project

The overview should cover the background information about the project, the substantive issues being investigated, and the relevant readings about the issues.

- Define a practice put into place at the school 2 or more years ago, aimed
  directly at improving school instruction; does the practice have a name?
    Operationalize the practice by placing the actions and events into a
    logic model framework; collect information about the chronology of
    these actions and events, as well as their causal relations
    Collect data related to the nature and extent of any improvements for
    the relevant period of time—for example,
       Raised expectations or consensus over goals
       Improved educational standards or tightened academic requirements
       Increased quality of the teaching staff
       Increased participation by parents in their child's learning
       Student performance (e.g., enrollment in specific courses,
       attendance, or results from achievement tests)

Figure 3.3   An Illustrative Protocol Question (From a Study of School
                 Practices)

As for background information, every project has its own context and
perspective. Some projects, for instance, are funded by government agencies
having a general mission and clientele that need to be remembered in conducting the research. Other projects have broader theoretical concerns or are
offshoots of earlier research studies. Whatever the situation, this type of
background information, in summary form, belongs in the overview section.

A procedural element of this background section is a statement about the
project that you can present to anyone who may want to know about the
project, its purpose, and the people involved in conducting and sponsoring
the project. This statement can even be accompanied by a letter of introduction, to be sent to all major interviewees and organizations that may be
the subject of a study. (See Figure 3.4 for an illustrative letter.) The bulk of
the overview, however, should be devoted to the substantive issues being
investigated. This may include the rationale for selecting the sites, the
propositions or hypotheses being examined, and the broader theoretical or
policy relevance of the inquiry. For all of these topics, relevant readings
should be cited, and the essential reading materials should be made available to everyone on the case study team.

A good overview will communicate to the informed reader (i.e., someone familiar with the general topic of inquiry) the case study's purpose and
setting. Some of the materials (such as a summary describing the project)
may be needed for other purposes anyway, so that writing the overview
should be seen as a doubly worthwhile activity. In the same vein, a

NATIONAL COMMISSION ON NEIGHBORHOODS
2000 K Street, N.W., Suite 350
Washington, D.C. 20006
202-632-5200

May 30, 1978

To Whom It May Concern:

This is to introduce
a highly qualified individual with wide experience
in the field of neighborhood revitalization and community organization.   has been engaged
by the National Commission on Neighborhoods to join
a team of experts now undertaking a series of 40-50
case studies commissioned by our Task Force on Gover-
nance.

Ultimately, by means of this case study
approach, the Commission hopes to identify and document answers to such questions as: What enables some
neighborhoods to survive, given the forces, attitudes
and investment policies (both public and private)
working against them? What preconditions are necessary in order to expand the number of neighborhoods
where successful revitalization, benefiting existing
residents, is possible? What can be done to promote
these preconditions?

This letter is directed to community leaders,
administrative staff and city officials. We must ask
you to give your time, experience and patience to our
interviewers. Your cooperation is most essential if
the case studies are to successfully guide and support
the final policy recommendations which the Commission
must forward to the President and to Congress.

On behalf of all twenty members of the Commission,
I wish to express our gratitude for your assistance.
Should you wish to be entered on our mailing list for
the Commission newsletter and final report, our interviewer will be glad to make the proper arrangements.

Again, thank you very much.

Sincerely,

/signed/
Senator Joseph F. Timilty
Chairman

Figure 3.4   Illustrative Letter of Introduction

well-conceived overview even may later form the basis for the background and introduction to the final case study report.

Field Procedures

Chapter 1 has previously defined case studies as studies of events within their real-life context. This has important implications for defining and designing the case study, which have been discussed in Chapters 1 and 2.

For data collection, however, this characteristic of case studies also raises an important issue, for which properly designed field procedures are essential. You will be collecting data from people and institutions in their everyday situations, not within the controlled confines of a laboratory, the sanctity of a library, or the structured limitations of a rigid questionnaire. In a case study, you must therefore learn to integrate real-world events with the needs of the data collection plan. In this sense, you do not have the control over the data collection environment as others might have in using the other research strategies discussed in Chapter 1.

Note that in a laboratory experiment, human "subjects" are solicited to enter into the laboratory—an environment controlled nearly entirely by the research investigator. The subject, within ethical and physical constraints, must follow the instructions of the investigator, which carefully prescribe the desired behavior. Similarly, the human "respondent" to a survey questionnaire cannot deviate from the agenda set by the questions. The respondent's behavior is constrained by the ground rules of the investigator. (Of course, the subject or respondent who does not wish to follow the prescribed behaviors may freely drop out of the experiment or survey.) Finally, in the historical archive, pertinent documents may not always be available, but the investigator can inspect what exists at his or her own pace and at a time convenient to his or her schedule. In all three situations, the research investigator closely controls the formal data collection activity.

Doing case studies involves an entirely different situation. For interviewing key persons, you must cater to the interviewee's schedule and availability, not your own. The nature of the interview is much more open-ended, and an interviewee may not necessarily cooperate fully in answering the questions. Similarly, in making observations of real-life activities, you are intruding into the world of the subject being studied rather than the reverse; under these conditions, you are the one who may have to make special arrangements to be able to act as an observer (or even as a participant-observer). As a result, your behavior—and not that of the subject or respondent—is the one likely to be constrained.

This contrasting process of doing data collection leads to the need to have explicit and well-planned field procedures encompassing guidelines for "coping" behaviors. Imagine, for instance, sending a youngster to camp; because you do not know what to expect, the best preparation is to have the resources to be prepared. Case study field procedures should be the same way.

With this orientation in mind, the field procedures of the protocol need to emphasize the major tasks in collecting data, including the following:

- Gaining access to key organizations or interviewees
- Having sufficient resources while in the field—including a personal computer, writing instruments, paper, paper clips, and a preestablished quiet place to write notes privately
- Developing a procedure for calling for assistance and guidance, if needed, from other case study investigators or colleagues
- Making a clear schedule of the data collection activities that are expected to be completed within specified periods of time
- Providing for unanticipated events, including changes in the availability of interviewees as well as changes in the mood and motivation of the case study investigator

These are the types of topics that can be included in the field procedures section of the protocol. Depending on the type of study being done, the specific procedures will vary.

The more operational these procedures are, the better. To take but one minor issue as an example, case study data collection frequently results in the accumulation of numerous documents at the field site. The burden of carrying such bulky documents can be reduced by two procedures. First, the case study team may have had the foresight to bring large, prelabeled envelopes, allowing the team to mail the documents back to the office rather than carry them. Second, field time may have been set aside for perusing the documents and then going to a local copier facility and copying only the few relevant pages of each document—and then returning the original documents to the informants at the field site. These and other operational details can enhance the overall quality and efficiency of case study data collection.

Case Study Questions

The heart of the protocol is a set of substantive questions reflecting your actual line of inquiry. Two characteristics distinguish these questions from those in a survey interview. (Refer back to Figure 3.3 for an illustrative question from a study of a school program; the complete protocol included dozens of such questions.)

General orientation of questions. First, the questions are posed *to you, the investigator,* not to an interviewee. In this sense, the protocol is directed at an entirely different party than a survey instrument. The protocol's questions, in essence, are your reminders regarding the information that needs to be collected and why. In some instances, the specific questions also may serve as prompts in asking questions during a case study interview; however, the main purpose of the protocol's questions is to keep the investigator on track as data collection proceeds.

Each question should be accompanied by a list of likely sources of evidence. Such sources may include the names of individual interviewees, documents, or observations. This crosswalk between the questions of interest and the likely sources of evidence is extremely helpful in collecting case study data. Before starting a particular interview, for instance, a case study investigator can quickly review the major questions that the interview should cover. (Again, these questions form the structure of the inquiry and are not intended as the literal questions to be asked of the interviewee.)

Levels of questions. Second, the questions in the case study protocol should reflect the full set of concerns from the initial design. The questions can, remarkably, occur at any of five levels:

Level 1: questions asked of specific interviewees

Level 2: questions asked of the individual case (these are the questions in the case study protocol to be answered by the investigator during a single case, even when the single case is part of a larger, multiple-case study)

Level 3: questions asked of the pattern of findings across multiple cases

Level 4: questions asked of an entire study—for example, calling on information beyond the case study evidence and including other literature or published data that may have been reviewed

Level 5: normative questions about policy recommendations and conclusions, going beyond the narrow scope of the study

Of these five levels, you only should articulate Level 1 and Level 2 questions for data collection purposes (the role of Levels 3, 4, and 5 is clarified later).

Furthermore, the difference between Level 1 and Level 2 questions is highly significant. The two types of questions are most commonly confused because investigators think that their questions of inquiry (Level 2) are synonymous with the specific questions they will ask in the field (Level 1). To disentangle these two levels in your own mind, think again about a detective, especially a wily one. The detective has in mind what the course of events in a crime might have been (Level 2), but the actual questions posed to any witness or suspect (Level 1) do not necessarily betray the detective's thinking. The *verbal* line of inquiry is different from the *mental* line of inquiry, and this is the difference between Level 1 and Level 2 questions. For the case study protocol, explicitly articulating the Level 2 questions is therefore of much greater importance than any attempt to identify the Level 1 questions.

The other levels also should be understood clearly. A cross-case question, for instance (Level 3), may be whether larger school districts are more responsive than smaller school districts or whether complex bureaucratic structures make the larger districts more cumbersome and less responsive. However, this Level 3 question should not be part of the protocol for collecting data from the single case because the single case can address only the responsiveness of a single school district. The Level 3 question cannot be addressed until the data from all the single cases (in a multiple-case study) are examined. Thus, only the multiple-case analysis can cover Level 3 questions. Similarly, the questions at Levels 4 and 5 also go well beyond any individual case study, and you should note this limitation when including such questions in the case study protocol. Remember: *The protocol is for the data collection from a single case (even when part of a multiple-case study) and is not intended to serve the entire project.*

Other data collection devices. The protocol questions also can include empty "table shells" (for more detail, see Miles & Huberman, 1994). These are the outlines of a table, defining precisely the "rows" and "columns" of a data array—but in the absence of having the actual data. In this sense, the table shell indicates the data to be collected, and your job is to collect the data called forth by the table. Such table shells help in several ways. First, the table shells force you to identify exactly what data are being sought. Second, they ensure that parallel information will be collected at different sites where a multiple-case design is being used. Finally, the table shells aid in understanding what will be done with the data once they have been collected.

Undesired confusion between unit of data collection and unit of analysis. A more subtle and serious problem also can arise in articulating the questions in a case study protocol. The questions may cater to the units of data

Figure 3.5   Design Versus Data Collection: Different Units of Analysis
SOURCE: COSMOS Corporation.

collection, which may be at a different level from the unit of analysis of the case study. Confusion will occur if, under these circumstances, the data collection process leads to an (undesirable) change in the unit of analysis.

The common confusion begins because the data collection sources may be individual people (e.g., interviews with individuals), whereas the unit of analysis of your case study may be organizational (e.g., the organization to which the individual belongs)—a frequent design when the case study is about an organization. Even though your data collection may have to rely heavily on information from individual interviewees, your conclusions cannot be based entirely on interviews as a source of information (you would then have collected information about individuals' reports about the organization, not necessarily about organizational events as they actually had occurred).

However, the reverse situation also can be true. Your case study may be about an individual, but the sources of information can include archival records (e.g., personnel files or student records) from the organization. In this situation, you also would want to avoid basing your conclusions about the individual from the organizational sources of information only. Figure 3.5 illustrates these two situations, in which the unit of analysis for the case study is different from the unit of analysis of the data collection source.

Guide for the Case Study Report

This element is generally missing in most case study plans. Investigators neglect to think about the outline, format, or audience for the case study report until after the data have been collected. Yet some planning at this preparatory stage—admittedly out of sequence in the typical conduct of most research—means that a tentative outline can (and should) appear in the case study protocol. (Chapter 6 of this book discusses the possible structure of a case study report in detail.)

Again, one reason for the traditional, linear sequence is related to practices with other research strategies. One does not worry about the report from an experiment until after the experiment has been completed because the format of the report and its likely audience are going to be dictated by an academic journal. Most reports of experiments follow a similar outline: the posing of the research questions and hypotheses; a description of the research design, apparatus, and data collection procedures; the presentation of the data collected; the analysis of the data; and a discussion of findings and conclusions.

Unfortunately, case study reports do not have such a uniformly acceptable outline. Nor, in many instances, do case study reports end up in journals (Feagin et al., 1991, pp. 269-273). For this reason, each investigator must be concerned, throughout the conduct of a case study, with the design of the final case study report. The problem is not easy to deal with.

In addition, the protocol also can indicate the extent of documentation for the case study report. Properly done, the data collection is likely to lead to large amounts of documentary evidence, taking the form of published reports, publications, memoranda, and other documents collected about the case. What is to be done with this documentation for later presentation? In most studies, the documents are filed away and seldom retrieved. Yet this documentation is an important part of the "database" for a case study (see Chapter 4) and should not be ignored until after the case study has been completed. One possibility is to have the case study report include an annotated bibliography in which each of the available documents is itemized. The annotations would help a reader (or the investigator, at some later date) to know which documents might be relevant for further inquiry.

In summary, to the extent possible, the basic outline of the case study report should be part of the protocol. This will facilitate the collection of relevant data, in the appropriate format, and will reduce the possibility that a return visit to the case study site will be necessary. At the same time, the existence of such an outline should not imply rigid adherence to a predesigned protocol. In fact, case study plans can change as a result of the initial data collection, and you are encouraged to consider these flexibilities—if used properly and without bias—to be an advantage of the case study strategy.

SCREENING CASE STUDY NOMINATIONS

Another preparatory step is the final selection of the "sites" or individuals who will serve as your case studies. Sometimes, the selection is straightforward because you have chosen to study a unique case whose identity has been known from the outset of your inquiry. Or, you already may know the case you will study because of some special arrangement or access that you have. However, at other times, there may be many qualified case study candidates, and you must choose your final single case or array of multiple cases from among them. The goal of the screening procedure is to be sure that you identify cases properly prior to formal data collection. The worst scenario would occur when, after having started formal data collection, the case turns out not to be viable or to represent an instance of something other than what you had intended to study.

When you have only a score or so (20 to 30) of possible candidates that can serve as your case studies (whether these candidates are "sites" or individuals or some other entity depends on your unit of analysis), the screening may consist of querying people knowledgeable about each candidate. You even may collect limited documentation about each candidate. To be avoided, at all costs, is an extensive screening procedure that effectively becomes a "mini" case study in effort. Prior to collecting the screening data, you should have defined a set of operational criteria whereby candidates will be deemed qualified to serve as cases. Then you should select randomly from the qualified candidates, whether comprising all or only a subgroup of the original candidates.

When the eligible number of candidates is larger, a two-stage screening procedure is warranted. The first stage should consist of collecting relevant quantitative data about the entire pool from some archival source (e.g., statistical databases about individual schools or firms). You may have to obtain the archival data from some central source (e.g., a federal, state, or local agency or a national association). Once obtained, you should define some relevant criteria for either stratifying or reducing the number of candidates. The goal is to reduce the number of candidates to 20 to 30 and then to conduct the second screening stage, which consists of carrying out the procedure in the previous paragraph.

In completing the screening process, you may want to revisit your earlier decision about the total number of cases to be studied. Regardless of any resource constraints, if multiple candidates are qualified to serve as cases, the larger the number you can study, the better.

THE PILOT CASE STUDY

A final preparation for data collection is the conduct of a pilot case study. The pilot case may be chosen for several reasons unrelated to the criteria for selecting the final cases in the case study design. For example, the informants at the pilot site may be unusually congenial and accessible, or the site may be geographically convenient or may have an unusual amount of documentation and data. One other possibility is that the pilot case represents a most complicated case, compared to the likely real cases, so that nearly all relevant data collection issues will be encountered in the pilot case.

The pilot case study will help you to refine your data collection plans with respect to both the content of the data and the procedures to be followed. In this regard, it is important to note that a *pilot test* is not a *pretest*. The pilot case is more formative, assisting you to develop relevant lines of questions—possibly even providing some conceptual clarification for the research design as well. In contrast, the pretest is the occasion for a formal "dress rehearsal," in which the data collection plan is used as the final plan as faithfully as possible.

The pilot case study can be so important that more resources may be devoted to this phase of the research than to the collection of data from any of the actual cases. For this reason, several subtopics are worth further discussion: the selection of pilot cases, the nature of the inquiry for the pilot cases, and the nature of the reports from the pilot cases.

Selection of Pilot Cases

In general, convenience, access, and geographic proximity can be the main criteria for selecting the pilot case or cases. This will allow for a less structured and more prolonged relationship to develop between the interviewees and the case study investigator than might occur in the "real" case study sites. The pilot site could then assume the role of a "laboratory" for the investigators, allowing them to observe different phenomena from many different angles or to try different approaches on a trial basis.

One study of technological innovations in local services (Yin, 1979, 1981c) actually had seven pilot cases, each focusing on a different type of technology. Four of the cases were located in the same metropolitan area as the research team's and were visited first. Three of the cases, however, were located in different cities and were the basis for a second set of visits. The cases were not chosen because of their distinctive technologies or for any other substantive reason. The main criterion, besides proximity, was the fact that access to the sites was made easy by some prior personal contact on the part of the research team. Finally, the interviewees at the sites also were congenial to the notion that the investigators were at an early stage of their research and would not have a fixed agenda.

Nature of the Pilot Inquiry

The inquiry for the pilot case can be much broader and less focused than the ultimate data collection plan. Moreover, the inquiry can cover both substantive and methodological issues.

In the above-mentioned example, the research team used the seven pilot cases to improve its conceptualization of different types of technologies and their related organizational effects. The pilot studies were done prior to the selection of specific technologies for the final data collection—and prior to the final articulation of the study's theoretical propositions. Thus, the pilot data provided considerable insight into the basic issues being studied. This information was used in parallel with an ongoing review of relevant literature, so that the final research design was informed both by prevailing theories and by a fresh set of empirical observations. The dual sources of information help to ensure that the actual study reflected significant theoretical or policy issues as well as questions relevant to contemporary cases.

Methodologically, the work at the pilot sites can provide information about relevant field questions and about the logistics of the field inquiry. In the technology pilot sites, one important logistical question was whether to observe the technology in action first or to collect information about the prevalent organizational issues first. This choice interacted with a further question about the deployment of the field team: If the team consisted of two or more persons, what assignments required the team to work together and what assignments could be completed separately? Variations in these procedures were tried during the pilot case studies, the trade-offs were acknowledged, and eventually a satisfactory procedure was developed for the formal data collection plan.

Reports From the Pilot Cases

The pilot case reports are mainly of value to the investigators and need to be written clearly, even if in the form of memoranda. One difference between the pilot reports and the actual case study reports is that the pilot reports should be explicit about the lessons learned for both research design and field procedures. The pilot reports might even contain subsections on these topics.

If more than a single pilot case is planned, the report from one pilot case also can indicate the modifications to be attempted in the next pilot case. In other words, the report can contain the agenda for the ensuing pilot case. If enough pilot cases are done in this manner, the final agenda may actually become a good prototype for the final case study protocol.

SUMMARY

This chapter has reviewed the preparations for data collection. Depending on the scope of a case study—whether single or multiple sites will be involved or whether single or multiple investigators will be involved—the preparatory tasks will be correspondingly straightforward or complex.

The major topics have been the desired skills of the case study investigator, the preparation and training of the case study investigators for a specific case study, the nature of the case study protocol, the screening of candidate cases, and the role and purpose of a pilot case study. Every case study should follow these different steps to varying degrees, depending on the specific inquiry.

As with the management of other affairs, the expertise with which these activities is conducted will improve with practice. Thus, one desirable sequence is for you to complete a relatively straightforward case study before attempting to do a more complex one from a managerial standpoint. With the successful completion of each case study, these preparatory tasks may even become second nature. Furthermore, if the same case study team has conducted several different studies together, the team will work with increasing efficiency and professional satisfaction with each ensuing case study.

EXERCISES

1. *Identifying skills for doing case studies.* Name the various skills that are important for a case study investigator to have. Do you know any people who have been successful in doing case study research? What strengths and weaknesses do they have as research investigators? Are these similar to the ones you have just named?

2. *Retrospectively developing an "old" protocol.* Select one of the case studies cited in the BOXES of this book. For just one of the chapters in this case study, design the protocol that would have yielded the findings now found in the chapter. What questions would have been posed by the protocol? What procedures followed in answering these questions and collecting the relevant data?

3. *Developing a "new" protocol.* Select some phenomenon in need of explanation from your university's everyday life. Illustrative topics might be, for example, why the university recently changed some policy or how your department makes decisions about its curriculum requirements. For this phenomenon, design a case study protocol to collect the information needed to make an adequate explanation. Whom would you interview? What documents would you seek? What observations, if any, would you make? How would all of these relate to the key questions of your case study?

4. *Conducting training for case study research.* Describe the major ways in which the preparation and training to do a case study project are *different* from those for doing projects using other types of research strategies (e.g., surveys, experiments, histories, and archival analysis). Develop a training agenda to prepare for a case study you might be considering, in which two or three persons are to collaborate.

5. *Selecting a case for doing a pilot study.* Define the desired features for a pilot case as a prelude to a new case study research project. How would you go about contacting and using such a case? Describe why you might want only one pilot site, as opposed to two or more pilot sites.

NOTE

1. The difference between having a single case study investigator and needing multiple investigators can create a significantly different orientation to the entire case study method. The classic single investigators have frequently been brilliant and creative—quickly and intuitively adapting to new conditions during data collection or finding newly appealing patterns during data analysis. With multiple investigators, such talents may have to be curbed because of the need for consistency across investigators, but the good discipline is rewarded by minimizing the likelihood of introducing bias into the case study.

4

Conducting Case Studies: Collecting the Evidence

Evidence for case studies may come from six sources: documents, archival records, interviews, direct observation, participant-observation, and physical artifacts. An investigator must know how to use these six sources, which call for knowing different methodological procedures.

In addition to the attention given to these individual sources, some overriding principles are important to any data collection effort in doing case studies. These include the use of (a) multiple sources of evidence (evidence from two or more sources, but converging on the same set of facts or findings), (b) a case study database (a formal assembly of evidence distinct from the final case study report), and (c) a chain of evidence (explicit links between the questions asked, the data collected, and the conclusions drawn). The incorporation of these principles into a case study investigation will increase its quality substantially.

Data for case studies can come from many sources of evidence. Six important ones are discussed in this chapter: documentation, archival records, interviews, direct observation, participant-observation, and physical artifacts. One purpose of this chapter is to review the six sources briefly. A second purpose is to convey three essential data collection principles, regardless of the sources used.

Supporting textbooks. You may find the six sources of evidence all potentially relevant, even in doing the same case study. For this reason, having them briefly reviewed, all in one place, may be helpful. For any given source of evidence, extensive further detail is available in numerous methodological textbooks and articles. Therefore, you also may want to check out some of these texts, especially if any single source of evidence is especially important to your case study. However, choosing among the texts and other works will require some searching and careful selection.

First, at an earlier time, guidance on collecting data relevant for case studies was available under three rubrics. One was "fieldwork" (e.g., Murphy, 1980; Wax, 1971), and a second was "field research" (e.g.,

Bouchard, 1976; Schatzman & Strauss, 1973). The third was "social science methods" more broadly (e.g., Kidder & Judd, 1986; Webb, Campbell, Schwartz, Sechrest, & Grove, 1981). Under these rubrics, the books also could cover the logistics of planning and conducting the fieldwork (e.g., Fiedler, 1978). The array of data collection techniques included under these rubrics was relevant to doing case studies, although none focused on case studies. The texts are still valuable because they are easy to use and discuss the basic data collection procedures to be followed. Unfortunately, due to their age the texts are probably increasingly hard to locate.

Second, recent texts are more readily available, but your choices are more complicated. Contemporary texts usually only cover some of the sources of evidence (e.g., single interviews, focus group interviews, and field observations) but not the others (e.g., archival and documentary sources), thereby losing the flavor of the entire blend of multiple sources. Furthermore, the texts also may not suit your needs because they may have a dominant substantive or disciplinary orientation, such as (a) clinical research or research on primary care settings (e.g., Crabtree & Miller, 1999), (b) program evaluations (e.g., Patton, 1990), or (c) social work research (e.g., Rubin & Babbie, 1993). Yet other texts may not have such an orientation, but they may focus on only a single source of evidence, such as field interviewing (e.g., Rubin & Rubin, 1995), doing participant-observation (e.g., Jorgensen, 1989), or using documentary evidence (e.g., Barzun & Graff, 1985). In general, contemporary texts appear to have become more specialized, and few span the needed breadth of data collection methods. In particular, few texts combine data collection through communicative and observational means (i.e., interviews and direct observations, including the use of videotapes) with data collection through documentary and archival sources.

Third, books that might at first appear to be comprehensive methodological texts also cover many topics in addition to data collection and, as a result, only devote a fraction of their entire text to data collection procedures (e.g., 1 of 11 chapters in Creswell, 1998; 1 of 26 chapters in Silverman, 2000). Other books that do have a truly comprehensive range and that do discuss data collection techniques in greater detail are nevertheless designed to serve more as reference works than as textbooks to be used by individual investigators (e.g., Bickman & Rog, 2000).

Given these variations, you must overcome the complex if not fragmented nature of the methodological marketplace represented by these texts. To do so will make your own data collection procedures even better.

Supporting principles. In addition to being familiar with the data collection procedures using the six different sources of evidence, you also need to continue addressing the design challenges enumerated in Chapter 2: construct validity, internal validity, external validity, and reliability. For this reason, this chapter gives much emphasis to its second purpose, the discussion of three principles of data collection.

These principles have been neglected in the past and are discussed at length: (a) using multiple, not just single, sources of evidence; (b) creating a case study database; and (c) maintaining a chain of evidence. The principles are extremely important for doing high-quality case studies, are relevant to all six types of sources of evidence, and should be followed whenever possible. In particular, the principles, as noted in Chapter 2 (see Figure 2.5), will help to deal with the problems of construct validity and reliability.

SIX SOURCES OF EVIDENCE

The sources of evidence discussed here are the ones most commonly used in doing case studies: documentation, archival records, interviews, direct observations, participant-observation, and physical artifacts. However, you should be aware that a complete list of sources can be quite extensive—including films, photographs, and videotapes; projective techniques and psychological testing; proxemics; kinesics; "street" ethnography; and life histories (Marshall & Rossman, 1989).

A useful overview of the six major sources considers their comparative strengths and weaknesses (see Figure 4.1). You should immediately note that no single source has a complete advantage over all the others. In fact, the various sources are highly complementary, and a good case study will therefore want to use as many sources as possible (see the later discussion in this chapter on "multiple sources of evidence").

Documentation

Except for studies of preliterate societies,[1] documentary information is likely to be relevant to every case study topic. This type of information can take many forms and should be the object of explicit data collection plans. For instance, consider the following variety of documents:

- Letters, memoranda, and other communiques
- Agendas, announcements and minutes of meetings, and other written reports of events

Source of Evidence	Strengths	Weaknesses
Documentation	• stable—can be reviewed repeatedly • unobtrusive—not created as a result of the case study • exact—contains exact names, references, and details of an event • broad coverage—long span of time, many events, and many settings	• retrievability—can be low • biased selectivity, if collection is incomplete • reporting bias—reflects (unknown) bias of author • access—may be deliberately blocked
Archival Records	• *[Same as above for documentation]* • precise and quantitative	• *[Same as above for documentation]* • accessibility due to privacy reasons
Interviews	• targeted—focuses directly on case study topic • insightful—provides perceived causal inferences	• bias due to poorly constructed questions • response bias • inaccuracies due to poor recall • reflexivity—interviewee gives what interviewer wants to hear
Direct Observations	• reality—covers events in real time • contextual—covers context of event	• time-consuming • selectivity—unless broad coverage • reflexivity—event may proceed differently because it is being observed • cost—hours needed by human observers
Participant-Observation	• *[Same as above for direct observations]* • insightful into interpersonal behavior and motives	• *[Same as above for direct observations]* • bias due to investigator's manipulation of events
Physical Artifacts	• insightful into cultural features • insightful into technical operations	• selectivity • availability

Figure 4.1   Six Sources of Evidence: Strengths and Weaknesses

- Administrative documents—proposals, progress reports, and other internal records
- Formal studies or evaluations of the same "site" under study
- Newspaper clippings and other articles appearing in the mass media or in community newsletters

These and other types of documents are useful even though they are not always accurate and may not be lacking in bias. In fact, documents must be carefully used and should not be accepted as literal recordings of events that have taken place. Few people realize, for instance, that even the "verbatim" transcripts of official U.S. Congress hearings have been deliberately edited—by the congressional staff and others who may have testified—before being printed in final form. In another field, historians working with primary documents also must be concerned with the validity of a document.

For case studies, the most important use of documents is to corroborate and augment evidence from other sources. First, documents are helpful in verifying the correct spellings and titles or names of organizations that might have been mentioned in an interview. Second, documents can provide other specific details to corroborate information from other sources. If the documentary evidence is contradictory rather than corroboratory, you need to pursue the problem by inquiring further into the topic. Third, you can make inferences from documents—for example, by observing the distribution list for a specific document, you may find new questions about communications and networking within an organization. However, you should treat inferences only as clues worthy of further investigation rather than as definitive findings because the inferences could later turn out to be false leads.

Because of their overall value, documents play an explicit role in any data collection in doing case studies. Systematic searches for relevant documents are important in any data collection plan. For example, during field visits, you should allot time for using local libraries and other reference centers. You should also arrange access to examine the files of any organizations being studied, including a review of documents that may have been put into cold storage. The scheduling of such retrieval activities is usually a flexible matter, independent of other data collection activities, and the search can usually be conducted at your convenience. For this reason, there is little excuse for omitting a thorough review of documentary evidence. Among such evidence, newspaper accounts are excellent sources for covering certain topics, such as the two in BOXES 15 and 16.

At the same time, many people have been critical of the potential over-reliance on documents in case study research. This is probably because the casual investigator may mistakenly assume that all kinds of documents—including proposals for projects or programs—contain the unmitigated truth. In fact, you need to remember that every document was written for some specific purpose and some specific audience *other than* those of the case study being done. In this sense, the case study investigator is a vicarious observer, and the documentary evidence reflects a communication among other parties attempting to achieve some other objectives. By

---

BOX 15

**Combining Personal Participation
With Extensive Newspaper Documentation**

Improving educational conditions—especially for urban schools in the United States—has become one of the biggest challenges for the 21st century. How the Houston, Texas, system dealt with constrained fiscal resources, diverse student populations, and local political constituencies is the topic of an exciting and riveting case study by Donald McAdams (2000). McAdams benefits from having been a member of the system's school board for three elected, 4-year terms. He writes as a storyteller, not a social science analyst. At the same time, the book contains numerous references to local newspaper articles to corroborate events. The result is one of the most readable but also well-documented case studies readers will encounter.

BOX 16

Using Documentary Sources to Reconstruct Reality

R. N. Jacobs (1996) shows how two different local newspapers constructed different perspectives on the *meaning* of a now well-known civil rights "case"—the beating of Rodney King in Los Angeles. Jacobs's "case" is not the civil rights case. Rather, the study is about how different narrative constructions (by two different newspapers, based on an analysis of 357 articles in one newspaper and 137 in the other) can affect the selection and interpretation of significant crises. As such, Jacobs's case also can be used to alert case study investigators about the potential biases of documentary evidence and how such biases might be addressed.

---

constantly trying to identify these objectives, you are less likely to be misled by documentary evidence and more likely to be correctly critical in interpreting the contents of such evidence.[2]

Archival Records

For many case studies, archival records—often taking the form of computer files and records—also may be relevant. Examples of archival records include the following:

- *Service records,* such as those showing the number of clients served over a given period of time

- *Organizational records,* such as organizational charts and budgets over a period of time

- *Maps and charts* of the geographical characteristics or layouts of a place

- *Lists* of names and other relevant items

- *Survey data,* such as census records or data previously collected about a "site"

- *Personal records,* such as diaries, calendars, and telephone listings

These and other archival records can be used in conjunction with other sources of information in producing a case study. However, unlike documentary evidence, the usefulness of these archival records will vary from case study to case study. For some studies, the records can be so important that they can become the object of extensive retrieval and quantitative analysis.[3] In other studies, they may be of only passing relevance.

When archival evidence has been deemed relevant, an investigator must be careful to ascertain the conditions under which it was produced as well as its accuracy. Sometimes, the archival records can be highly quantitative, but numbers alone should not automatically be considered a sign of accuracy. Nearly every social scientist, for instance, is aware of the pitfalls of using the FBI's Uniform Crime Reports—or any other archival records based on crimes reported by law enforcement agencies. The same general word of caution made earlier with documentary evidence therefore also applies to archival evidence: Most archival records were produced for a specific purpose and a specific audience (other than the case study investigation), and these conditions must be fully appreciated in interpreting the usefulness and accuracy of the records.

Interviews

One of the most important sources of case study information is the interview. Such an observation may be surprising because of the usual association between interviews and the survey method. However, interviews also are essential sources of case study information. The interviews will appear to be guided conversations rather than structured queries. In other words, although you will be pursuing a consistent line of inquiry, your actual stream of questions in a case study interview is likely to be fluid rather than rigid (Rubin & Rubin, 1995).

Note that this means that throughout the interview process, you have two jobs: (a) to follow your own line of inquiry, as reflected by your case study protocol, and (b) to ask your actual (conversational) questions in an unbiased manner that also serves the needs of your line of inquiry. For instance, you may want (in your line of inquiry) to know "why" a particular process occurred as it did. Becker (1998, pp. 58-60), however, has pointed to the important difference in actually posing a "why" question to an informant (which in his view creates defensiveness on the informant's part) in contrast to posing a "how" question—the latter, in fact, being his preferred way of addressing any "why" question in an actual conversation. Thus, case study interviews require you to operate on two levels at the same time: satisfying the needs of your line of inquiry while simultaneously putting forth "friendly" and "nonthreatening" questions in your open-ended interviews.

As a result, most commonly, case study interviews are of an *open-ended nature,* in which you can ask key respondents about the facts of a matter as well as their opinions about events. In some situations, you may even ask the respondent to propose his or her own insights into certain occurrences and may use such propositions as the basis for further inquiry. The respondent also can suggest other persons for you to interview, as well as other sources of evidence.

The more that a respondent assists in this manner, the more that the role may be considered one of an "informant" rather than a respondent. Key informants are often critical to the success of a case study. Such persons not only provide the case study investigator with insights into a matter but also can suggest sources of corroboratory or contrary evidence—and also initiate the access to such sources. Such a person, named "Doc," played an essential role in the conduct of the famous case study presented in *Street Corner Society* (Whyte, 1943/1955). Similar key informants have been noted in other case studies. Of course, you need to be cautious about becoming overly dependent on a key informant, especially because of the interpersonal influence—frequently subtle—that the informant may have over you. A reasonable way of dealing with this pitfall again is to rely on other sources of evidence to corroborate any insight by such informants and to search for contrary evidence as carefully as possible.

A second type of interview is a *focused interview* (Merton, Fiske, & Kendall, 1990), in which a respondent is interviewed for a short period of time—an hour, for example. In such cases, the interviews may still remain open-ended and assume a conversational manner, but you are more likely to be following a certain set of questions derived from the case study protocol.

For example, a major purpose of such an interview might simply be to corroborate certain facts that you already think have been established (but not to ask about other topics of a broader, open-ended nature). In this situation, the specific questions must be carefully worded, so that you appear

---

BOX 17

A Case Study Encompassing a Survey

Hanna (2000) used a variety of sources of data, including a survey, to conduct a case study of an urban-rural estuarine setting. In this setting, an integrated resource management program was established to help manage environmental and economic planning issues. The case study focused on the estuarine setting, including its description and the policies and public participation that appeared to affect it. Within the case study, participants in the policy process served as an embedded unit of analysis. Hanna surveyed these individuals, and the survey data were presented with statistical tests as part of the single-case study.

---

genuinely naive about the topic and allow the respondent to provide a fresh commentary about it; in contrast, if you ask leading questions, the corroboratory purpose of the interview will not have been served. Even so, you need to exercise caution when different interviewees appear to be echoing the same thoughts—corroborating each other but in a conspiratorial way.[4] Further probing is needed. One way is to test the sequence of events by deliberately checking with persons known to hold different perspectives. If one of the interviewees fails to comment, even though the others tend to corroborate one another's versions of what took place, the good case study investigator will even indicate this result by citing the fact that a person was asked but declined to comment, as done in good journalistic accounts.

Yet a third type of interview entails more structured questions, along the lines of a formal *survey.* Such a survey could be designed as part of a case study and produce quantitative data as part of the case study evidence (see BOX 17). This situation would be relevant, for instance, if you were doing a case study of an urban design project and surveyed a group of designers about the project (e.g., Crewe, 2001) or if you did a case study of an organization that included a survey of workers and managers. This type of survey would follow both the sampling procedures and the instruments used in regular surveys, and it would subsequently be analyzed in a similar manner. The difference would be the survey's role in relation to other sources of evidence. For example, residents' perceptions of neighborhood decline or improvement would not necessarily be taken as a measure of actual decline or improvement but would be considered only one component of the overall assessment of the neighborhood.

Overall, interviews are an essential source of case study evidence because most case studies are about human affairs. These human affairs should be reported and interpreted through the eyes of specific interviewees, and well-informed respondents can provide important insights into a situation. They also can provide shortcuts to the prior history of the situation, helping you to identify other relevant sources of evidence. However, the interviews should always be considered *verbal reports* only. As such, they are subject to the common problems of bias, poor recall, and poor or inaccurate articulation. Again, a reasonable approach is to corroborate interview data with information from other sources.

A common question about doing interviews is whether to record them. Using recording devices is in part a matter of personal preference. Audiotapes certainly provide a more accurate rendition of any interview than any other method. However, a recording device should not be used when (a) an interviewee refuses permission or appears uncomfortable in its presence, (b) there is no specific plan for transcribing or systematically listening to the contents of the electronic record—a process that takes enormous time and energy, (c) the investigator is clumsy enough with mechanical devices that the recording creates distractions during the interview itself, or (d) the investigator thinks that the recording device is a substitute for "listening" closely throughout the course of an interview.

Direct Observations

By making a field visit to the case study "site," you are creating the opportunity for direct observations. Assuming that the phenomena of interest have not been purely historical, some relevant behaviors or environmental conditions will be available for observation. Such observations serve as yet another source of evidence in a case study.

The observations can range from formal to casual data collection activities. Most formally, observational protocols can be developed as part of the case study protocol, and the field-worker may be asked to measure the incidence of certain types of behaviors during certain periods of time in the field (see BOX 18). This can involve observations of meetings, sidewalk activities, factory work, classrooms, and the like. Less formally, direct observations might be made throughout a field visit, including those occasions during which other evidence, such as that from interviews, is being collected. For instance, the condition of buildings or work spaces will indicate something about the climate or impoverishment of an organization; similarly, the location or the furnishings of a respondent's office may be one indicator of the status of the respondent within an organization.

BOX 18

Combining Formal Observations and Other Methods to Produce Quantitative and Qualitative Data for a Case Study

Case studies need not be limited to a single source of evidence. In fact, most of the better case studies rely on a variety of sources.

One example of a case study that used such a variety is a book by Gross et al. (1971), *Implementing Organizational Innovations,* covering events in a single school. The case study included an observational protocol for measuring the time that students spent on various tasks but also relied on a structured survey of a larger number of teachers, open-ended interviews with a smaller number of key persons, and a review of organizational documents. Both the observational and survey data led to quantitative information about attitudes and behavior in the school, whereas the open-ended interviews and documentary evidence led to qualitative information.

All sources of evidence were reviewed and analyzed together, so that the case study's findings were based on the convergence of information from different sources, not quantitative or qualitative data alone.

Observational evidence is often useful in providing additional information about the topic being studied. If a case study is about a new technology, for instance, observations of the technology at work are invaluable aids for understanding the actual uses of the technology or potential problems being encountered. Similarly, observations of a neighborhood or of an organizational unit add new dimensions for understanding either the context or the phenomenon being studied. The observations can be so valuable that you may even consider taking photographs at the case study site. At a minimum, these photographs will help to convey important case characteristics to outside observers (see Dabbs, 1982). Note, however, that in some situations—such as photographing students in public schools—you will need written permission before proceeding.

To increase the reliability of observational evidence, a common procedure is to have more than a single observer making an observation—whether of the formal or the casual variety. Thus, when resources permit, a case study investigation should allow for the use of multiple observers.

Participant-Observation

Participant-observation is a special mode of observation in which you are not merely a passive observer. Instead, you may assume a variety of roles within a case study situation and may actually participate in the events being studied. In urban neighborhoods, for instance, these roles may range from having casual social interactions with various residents to undertaking specific functional activities within the neighborhood (see Yin, 1982a). The roles for different illustrative studies in neighborhoods and organizations have included the following:

- Being a resident in a neighborhood that is the subject of a case study (see BOX 19)
- Taking some other functional role in a neighborhood, such as serving as a storekeeper's assistant
- Serving as a staff member in an organizational setting
- Being a key decision maker in an organizational setting

The participant-observation technique has been most frequently used in anthropological studies of different cultural or social groups. The technique also can be used in more everyday settings, such as a large organization (see BOX 20; also see BOX 15) or informal small groups.

Participant-observation provides certain unusual opportunities for collecting case study data, but it also involves major problems. The most distinctive opportunity is related to your ability to gain access to events or groups that are otherwise inaccessible to scientific investigation. In other words, for some topics, there may be no other way of collecting evidence than through participant-observation. Another distinctive opportunity is the ability to perceive reality from the viewpoint of someone "inside" the case study rather than external to it. Many have argued that such a perspective is invaluable in producing an "accurate" portrayal of a case study phenomenon. Finally, other opportunities arise because you may have the ability to manipulate minor events—such as convening a meeting of a group of persons in the case study. Only through participant-observation can such manipulation occur, as the use of documents, archival records, and interviews, for instance, all assume a passive investigator. The manipulations will not be as precise as those in experiments, but they can produce a greater variety of situations for the purposes of collecting data.

The major problems related to participant-observation have to do with the potential biases produced (see Becker, 1958). First, the investigator has less ability to work as an external observer and may, at times, have to assume positions or advocacy roles contrary to the interests of good scientific practice. Second, the participant-observer is likely to follow a commonly

BOX 19

Participant-Observation in a Neighborhood Near "Street Corner Society"

Participant-observation has been a method used frequently to study urban neighborhoods. One such study of subsequent fame was conducted by Herbert Gans (1962), who wrote *The Urban Villagers,* a study about "group and class in the life of Italian-Americans."

Gans's methodology is documented in a separate chapter of his book, titled "On the Methods Used in This Study." He notes that his evidence was based on six approaches: the use of the neighborhood's facilities, attendance at meetings, informal visiting with neighbors and friends, formal and informal interviewing, the use of informants, and direct observation. Of all these sources, the "participation role turned out to be most productive" (pp. 339-340). This role was based on Gans's being an actual resident, along with his wife, of the neighborhood he was studying. The result is a classic statement of neighborhood life undergoing urban renewal and change—a stark contrast to the stability found nearby, in Whyte's (1943/1955) *Street Corner Society,* some 20 years earlier.

BOX 20

A Participant-Observer Study in an "Everyday" Setting

Eric Redman (1973) provides an insider's account of how Congress works in his well-regarded case study, *The Dance of Legislation.* The case study traces the introduction and passage of the legislation that created the National Health Service Corps during the 91st Congress in 1970.

Redman's account, from the vantage point of an author who was also on the staff of one of the bill's main supporters, Senator Warren G. Magnuson, is not simply well written and easy to read. The account also provides the reader with great insight into the daily operations of Congress—from the introduction of a bill to its eventual passage, including the politics of a lame-duck session when Richard Nixon was president.

The account is an excellent example of participant-observation in a contemporary setting. It contains information about insiders' roles that few persons have been privileged to share. The subtle legislative strategies, the overlooked role of committee clerks and lobbyists, and the interaction between the legislative and executive branches of government are all recreated by the case study, and all add to the reader's general understanding of the legislative process.

known phenomenon and become a supporter of the group or organization being studied, if such support did not already exist. Third, the participant role may simply require too much attention relative to the observer role. Thus, the participant-observer may not have sufficient time to take notes or to raise questions about events from different perspectives, as a good observer might. Fourth, if the organization or social group being studied is physically dispersed, the participant-observer may find it difficult to be at the right place at the right time, either to participate in or to observe important events.

These trade-offs between the opportunities and the problems have to be considered seriously in undertaking any participant-observation study. Under some circumstances, this approach to case study evidence may be just the right approach; under other circumstances, the credibility of a whole case study project can be threatened.

Physical Artifacts

A final source of evidence is a physical or cultural artifact—a technological device, a tool or instrument, a work of art, or some other physical evidence. Such artifacts may be collected or observed as part of a field visit and have been used extensively in anthropological research.

Physical artifacts have less potential relevance in the most typical kind of case study. However, when relevant, the artifacts can be an important component in the overall case. For example, one case study of the use of personal computers in the classroom needed to ascertain the nature of the actual use of the machines. Although such use could be directly observed, an artifact—the computer printout—also was available. Students displayed these printouts as the finished product of their work and maintained notebooks of their printouts. Each printout showed not only the type of schoolwork that had been done but also the date and amount of computer time used to do the work. By examining the printouts, the case study investigators were able to develop a more precise understanding of the classroom applications over the length of an entire semester, far beyond that which could be directly observed in the limited time of a site visit.

Summary

This section has reviewed six commonly used sources of case study evidence. The procedures for collecting each type of evidence must be developed and mastered independently to ensure that each source is properly used. Not all sources will be relevant for all case studies. However, the trained case study investigator should be acquainted with the procedures associated with using each source of evidence—or have colleagues who have the needed expertise and who can work as members of the case study team.

THREE PRINCIPLES OF DATA COLLECTION

The benefits from these six sources of evidence can be maximized if you follow three principles. These principles are relevant to all six sources and, when used properly, can help to deal with the problems of establishing the construct validity and reliability of the case study evidence. The three are as follows.

Principle 1: Use Multiple Sources of Evidence

Any of the preceding sources of evidence can and have been the sole basis for entire studies. For example, some studies have relied only on participant-observation but have not examined a single document; similarly, numerous studies have relied on archival records but have not involved a single interview.

This isolated use of sources may be a function of the independent way that sources have typically been conceived—as if an investigator should choose the single most appropriate source or the one with which he or she is most familiar. Thus, on many an occasion, investigators have announced the design of a new study by identifying both the problem to be studied and the prior selection of a *single* source of evidence—such as "interviews"— as the focus of the data collection effort.

Triangulation: Rationale for using multiple sources of evidence. The approach to individual sources of evidence just described, however, is not recommended for conducting case studies. On the contrary, a major strength of case study data collection is the opportunity to use many different sources of evidence (see BOX 21, as well as BOX 18, for examples of such studies). Furthermore, the need to use multiple sources of evidence far exceeds that in other research strategies, such as experiments, surveys, or histories. Experiments, for instance, are largely limited to the measurement and recording of actual behavior in a laboratory and generally do not include the systematic use of survey or verbal information. Surveys tend to be the opposite, emphasizing verbal information but not the direct measurement or recording of individual behavior. Finally, histories are

---

BOX 21

**A Case Study Combining Personal Experience
With Extensive Field Research**

Most people across the country by now have heard of Head Start. Its development and growth into one of the most successful federal programs is traced by Zigler and Muenchow (1992). Their book is exceptionally insightful, possibly because it is based on Zigler's personal experiences with the program, beginning with his role as its first director. However, the book also is empirically based, with the coauthor contributing historical and field research, including interviews of more than 200 persons associated with Head Start. All of these multiple sources of evidence are integrated into a coherent if not compelling case study of Head Start. The result is a winning combination: a most readable but also well-documented book.

---

limited to events in the "dead" past and therefore seldom have any contemporary sources of evidence, such as direct observations of a phenomenon or interviews with key actors.

Of course, each of these strategies can be modified, creating hybrid strategies in which multiple sources of evidence are more likely to be relevant. An example of this is the evolution of "oral history" studies in the field of history. Nevertheless, such a modification of the traditional strategies does not alter the fact that the case study inherently deals with a wide variety of evidence, whereas the other strategies do not.

The use of multiple sources of evidence in case studies allows an investigator to address a broader range of historical, attitudinal, and behavioral issues. However, the most important advantage presented by using multiple sources of evidence is the development of *converging lines of inquiry,* a process of triangulation mentioned repeatedly in the previous section of this chapter. Thus, any finding or conclusion in a case study is likely to be much more convincing and accurate if it is based on several different sources of information, following a corroboratory mode (see BOX 22).

Patton (1987) discusses four types of triangulation in doing evaluations—the triangulation

1. of data sources (*data triangulation*),
2. among different evaluators (*investigator triangulation*),

---

BOX 22

Triangulating From Multiple Sources of Evidence

Basu, Dirsmith, and Gupta (1999) conducted a case study of the federal government's audit agency, the U.S. General Accounting Office. Their case was theory oriented and examined the relationship between an organization's actual work and the image it presents to external parties (the finding was that they are loosely coupled). The case study used an impressive array of sources of evidence—an extended period of field observations, with diaries; interviews of 55 persons; and reviews of historical accounts, public records, administrators' personal files, and news articles—all triangulating on the same set of research questions.

---

3. of perspectives to the same data set (*theory triangulation*), and

4. of methods (*methodological triangulation*).

The present discussion pertains only to the first of these four types (*data triangulation*), encouraging you to collect information from multiple sources but aimed at corroborating the same fact or phenomenon. In pursuing such corroboratory strategies, Figure 4.2 distinguishes between two conditions— 1) when you have really triangulated the data (upper portion) and 2) when you have multiple sources as part of the same study, but they nevertheless address *different* facts (lower portion). When you have really triangulated the data, the events or facts of the case study have been supported by more than a single source of evidence (e.g., Sieber, 1973; Yin, 1982c); when you have used multiple sources but not actually triangulated the data, you typically have analyzed each source of evidence separately and have compared the conclusions from the different analyses—but not triangulated the data.

With data triangulation, the potential problems of *construct validity* also can be addressed because the multiple sources of evidence essentially provide multiple measures of the same phenomenon. Not surprisingly, one analysis of case study methods found that those case studies using multiple sources of evidence were rated more highly, in terms of their overall quality, than those that relied on only single sources of information (see COSMOS, 1983).

Prerequisites for using multiple sources of evidence. At the same time, the use of multiple sources of evidence imposes a great burden, hinted at earlier, on yourself or any other case study investigator. First, the collection

CONVERGENCE OF EVIDENCE
(Single study)

NON CONVERGENCE OF EVIDENCE
(Separate substudies)

site visits ⟶ findings ⟶ conclusions

survey ⟶ findings ⟶ conclusions

documents ⟶ findings ⟶ conclusions
analysis

Figure 4.2 Convergence and Nonconvergence of Multiple Sources of Evidence
SOURCE: COSMOS Corporation.

of data from multiple sources is more expensive than if data were only collected from a single source (Denzin, 1978, p. 61). Second and more important, each investigator needs to know how to carry out the full variety of data collection techniques. For example, a case study investigator may have to collect and analyze documentary evidence as in history, to retrieve and analyze archival records as in economics or operations research, and to design and conduct surveys as in survey research. If any of these techniques is used improperly, the opportunity to address a broader array of issues or to establish converging lines of inquiry may be lost. This requirement for mastering multiple data collection techniques therefore raises important questions regarding the training and expertise of the case study investigator.

Unfortunately, many graduate training programs emphasize one type of data collection activity over all others, and the successful student is not likely to have a chance to master the others. To overcome such conditions, you should seek other ways of obtaining the needed training and practice. One such way is to work in a multidisciplinary research organization rather than being limited to a single academic department. Another way is to analyze the methodological writings of a variety of social scientists (see Hammond, 1968) and to learn the strengths and weaknesses of different data collection techniques as they have been practiced by experienced scholars. Yet a third way is to design different pilot studies that will provide an opportunity for practicing different techniques.

No matter how the experience is gained, every case study investigator should be well versed in a variety of data collection techniques so that a case study can use multiple sources of evidence. Without such multiple sources, an invaluable advantage of the case study strategy will have been lost.

Principle 2: Create a Case Study Database

A second principle has to do with the way of organizing and documenting the data collected for case studies. Here, case studies have much to borrow from the practices followed by the other research strategies defined in Chapter 1, whose documentation commonly consists of two *separate* collections:

1. the data or evidentiary base and
2. the report of the investigator, whether in article, report, or book form.

With the advent of computerized data files, the distinction between these two collections has been made even more clear. For example, investigators doing psychological, survey, or economic research may exchange data files and other electronic documentation that contain only the actual database— for example, behavioral responses or test scores in psychology, itemized responses to various survey questions, or economic indicators. The database can then be the subject of separate, secondary analysis, independent of any reports by the original investigator.

However, with case studies, the distinction between a separate database and the case study report has not yet become an institutionalized practice. Too often, the case study data are synonymous with the narrative presented in the case study report, and a critical reader has no recourse if he or she wants to inspect the raw data that led to the case study's conclusions. The case study report may not have presented adequate data, and without a case study database, the raw data may not be available for independent inspection. A major exception to this is when ethnographic studies have separated and stored data on their fieldwork, making these data available to new research investigators. The practice is sufficiently important, however, that every case study project should strive to develop a formal, presentable database, so that in principle, other investigators can review the evidence directly and not be limited to the written case study reports. In this manner, a case study database increases markedly the *reliability* of the entire case study.

The lack of a formal database for most case study efforts is a major shortcoming of case study research and needs to be corrected. There are numerous ways of accomplishing the task, as long as you and other investigators are aware of the need and are willing to commit the additional resources required to build the database. At the same time, the existence of an adequate database does not preclude the need to present sufficient evidence within the case study report itself (to be discussed further in Chapter 6). Every report should still contain enough data so that the reader of the report can draw independent conclusions about the case study.

Nevertheless, the initial problem of establishing a case study database has not been recognized by most of the books on field methods. Thus, the subsections below represent an extension of the current state of the art. The problem of developing the database is described in terms of four components: notes, documents, tabular materials, and narratives.

Case study notes. For case studies, notes are likely to be the most common component of a database. These notes take a variety of forms. The notes may be a result of an investigator's interviews, observations, or document analysis. The notes may be handwritten, typed, on audiotapes, or in computer files, and they may be assembled in the form of a diary, on index cards, or in some less organized fashion.

Regardless of their form or content, these case study notes must be stored in such a manner that other persons, including the investigator, can retrieve them efficiently at some later date. Most commonly, the notes can be divided into the major subjects—as outlined in the case study protocol— covered by a case study; however, any classificatory system will do, as long as the system is usable by an outside party. Only in this manner will the notes be available as part of the case study database.

This identification of the notes as part of the case study database does not mean, however, that the investigator needs to spend excessive amounts of time rewriting interviews or making extensive editorial changes to make the notes presentable. Such a building of a formal case record, including the editing and rewriting of interview notes, may be a misplaced priority. Any such editing effort should be directed at the case study report itself, not at the notes. The only essential characteristics of the notes are that they be organized, categorized, complete, and available for later access.

Case study documents. Many documents relevant to a case study will be collected during the course of a study. Chapter 3 indicated that the disposition of these documents should be covered in the case study protocol and suggested that one helpful way is to have an annotated bibliography of these documents. Such annotations would again facilitate storage and retrieval, so that later investigators can inspect or share the database.

The single, unique characteristic of these documents is that they are likely to require a large amount of physical storage space. In addition, the documents may be of varying importance to the database, and the investigator may want to establish a primary file and a secondary file for such documents. The main objective, again, is to make the documents readily retrievable for later inspection or perusal. In those instances when the documents have been relevant to specific interviews, one additional cross-reference is to have the interview notes cite the document.

Tabular materials. The database may consist of tabular materials, either collected from the site being studied or created by the research team. Such materials also need to be organized and stored to allow for later retrieval.

The materials may include survey and other quantitative data. For example, a survey may have been conducted at one or more of the case study sites as part of the overall study. In such situations, the tabular materials may even be stored in computer files. As another example, in dealing with archival or observational evidence, a case study may have called for "counts" of various phenomena (see Miles & Huberman, 1994). The documentation of these counts, done by the case study team, also should be organized and stored as part of the database. In brief, any tabular materials, whether based on surveys, observational counts, or archival data, can be treated in a manner similar to the way they are handled in applying other research methods.

Narratives. Certain types of narrative, produced by the case study investigator, also may be considered a formal part of the database and not part of the final case study report. This is reflected by a special practice that should be used more frequently: to have case study investigators compose *open-ended answers to the questions in the case study protocol.* This practice has been used on several occasions in multiple-case studies designed by the author (see BOX 23). The questions and answers, in modified form,

---

BOX 23

Narratives in the Case Study Database

A series of 12 case studies was done on personal computer use in schools (COSMOS, 1984b). Each case study was based on open-ended answers to about 50 protocol questions concerning matters such as the number and location of the personal computers (an inventory question requiring tabular and narrative responses), the relationship between the computer units and other computational systems within the school district, and the training and coordination provided by the school district.

The case study investigator's first responsibility was to answer these 50 questions as completely as possible, citing specific sources of evidence in footnotes. These answers were unedited, but they served as the basis for both the individual case reports and the cross-case analysis. The availability of the database meant that other members of the case study team could determine the events at each site, even before the case study reports were completed. These files remain a rich source of evidence that could be used again, even as part of another study.

---

can even serve directly as the basis for the final case study report, as described further in Chapter 6.

In such a situation, each answer represents an attempt to integrate the available evidence and to converge on the facts of the matter or their tentative interpretation. The process is actually an analytic one and is the start of the case study analysis. The format for the answers may be considered analogous to that of a comprehensive "take-home" exam, used in academic courses. The investigator is the respondent, and his or her goal is to cite the relevant evidence—whether from interviews, documents, observations, or archival evidence—in composing an adequate answer. The main purpose of the open-ended answer is to document the connection between specific pieces of evidence and various issues in the case study, generously using footnotes and citations.

The entire set of answers can be considered part of the case study database. The investigator, along with any other interested party, can then use this database to compose the actual case study report. Or, if no reports are composed concerning the individual cases (see Chapter 6 for such situations), the answers can serve as the database for the subsequent cross-case analysis.[5] Again, because the answers are part of the database and not of the final report, the investigators should not spend much time trying to make the answers presentable. In other words, they need not perform the standard editing and copyediting chores. The most important attribute of good answers is that they indeed connect the pertinent issues—through adequate citations—to specific evidence.

Principle 3: Maintain a Chain of Evidence

Another principle to be followed, to increase the *reliability* of the information in a case study, is to maintain a chain of evidence. Such a principle is based on a notion similar to that used in forensic investigations.

The principle is to allow an external observer—in this situation, the reader of the case study—to follow the derivation of any evidence, ranging from initial research questions to ultimate case study conclusions (see Figure 4.3). Moreover, this external observer should be able to trace the steps in either direction (from conclusions back to initial research questions or from questions to conclusions). As with criminological evidence, the process should be tight enough that evidence presented in "court"—the case study report—is assuredly the same evidence that was collected at the scene of the "crime" during the data collection process. Conversely, no original evidence should have been lost, through carelessness or bias, and therefore fail to receive appropriate attention in considering the "facts" of a case. If these objectives are achieved, a case study also will have addressed the methodological problem of determining construct validity, thereby increasing the overall quality of the case.

Imagine the following scenario. You have read the conclusions in a case study report and you want to know more about the basis for the conclusions. You therefore want to trace the evidentiary process backward.

First, the report itself should have made sufficient citation to the relevant portions of the case study database—for example, by citing specific documents, interviews, or observations. Second, the database, upon inspection, should reveal the actual evidence and also indicate the circumstances under which the evidence was collected—for example, the time and place of an interview. Third, these circumstances should be consistent with the specific procedures and questions contained in the case study protocol, to show that the data collection followed the procedures stipulated by the protocol. Finally, a reading of the protocol should indicate the link between the content of the protocol and the initial study questions.

In the aggregate, you have therefore been able to move from one part of the case study process to another, with clear cross-referencing to methodological procedures and to the resulting evidence. This is the ultimate "chain of evidence" that is desired.

Figure 4.3 Maintaining a Chain of Evidence
SOURCE: COSMOS Corporation.

SUMMARY

This chapter has reviewed six types of case study evidence, how they can be collected, and three important principles regarding the data collection process.

The data collection process for case studies is more complex than those used in other research strategies. The case study investigator must have a methodological versatility not necessarily required for using other strategies and must follow certain formal procedures to ensure *quality control* during the data collection process. The three principles described above are steps in this direction. They are not intended to straitjacket the inventive and insightful investigator. They are intended to make the process as explicit as possible, so that the final results—the data that have been collected—reflect a concern for construct validity and for reliability, thereby becoming worthy of further analysis. How such analysis can be carried out is the subject of the next chapter.

EXERCISES

1. *Using evidence.* Select one of the case studies cited in the BOXES of this book. Go through the case study, and identify five "facts" important to the case study. For each fact, indicate the source or sources of evidence, if any, used to define the fact. In how many instances was there more than a single source of evidence?

2. *Identifying illustrative types of evidence.* Name a case study topic you would like to study. For some aspect of this topic, identify the specific type of evidence that would be relevant—for example, if a document, what kind of document? If an interview, what respondent and what questions? If an archival record, what records and what variables?

3. *Seeking converging evidence.* Name a particular incident that occurred recently in your everyday life. How would you go about establishing the "facts" of this incident, if you wanted now (in retrospect) to demonstrate what had happened? Would you interview any important persons (including yourself)? Would there have been any artifacts or documentation to rely on?

4. *Practicing the development of a database.* For the topic you covered in the preceding question, write a short report (no more than two double-spaced pages). Start this report with the major question you were attempting to answer, and then provide the answer, citing the evidence you had used (your format should include footnotes). Envisage how this question-and-answer sequence might be one of many in your total case study "database."

5. *Establishing a chain of evidence.* State a hypothetical conclusion that might emerge from a case study you are going to do. Now work backward and identify the specific data or evidence that would have supported such a conclusion. Similarly, work backward and define the protocol question that would have led to the collection of this evidence, and then the study question that in turn would have led to the design of the protocol question. Do you understand how this chain of evidence has been formed and how one can move forward or backward in tracing the chain?

NOTES

1. Limited availability of print materials in low-income communities in the United States— including signage and materials in school and public libraries—has been the subject of study (Neuman & Celano, 2001). To the extent of such impoverishment, researchers studying such neighborhoods and their community organizations (or schools) may find the use of documentary sources of evidence also limited.

2. Excellent suggestions regarding the ways of verifying documentary evidence, including the nontrivial problem of determining the actual author of a document, are offered by Barzun and Graff (1986, pp. 109-133). An exemplary quantitative study of the authorship problem is found in Mosteller and Wallace (1984).

3. Chapter 9 of the companion book (Yin, 2003) contains a complete multiple-case study that quantitatively analyzed a critical set of archival records.

4. Such consistent responses are likely to occur when interviewing members of a "closed" institution, such as the residents of a drug treatment program or the teachers in a closely knit school. The apparent conspiracy arises because those being interviewed all are aware of the "socially desirable" responses and appear to be providing corroboratory evidence when in fact they are merely repeating their institution's mantra.

5. See Chapter 2 of the companion book (Yin, 2003) for an example of a complete case study that is written in the form of narrative answers to the protocol questions.

5

Analyzing Case Study Evidence

Data analysis consists of examining, categorizing, tabulating, testing, or otherwise recombining both quantitative and qualitative evidence to address the initial propositions of a study. Analyzing case study evidence is especially difficult because the strategies and techniques have not been well defined. Familiarity with various tools and manipulative techniques is helpful, but every case study should nevertheless strive to have a general analytic strategy—defining priorities for what to analyze and why. Three strategies are relying on theoretical propositions, setting up a framework based on rival explanations, and developing case descriptions.

Any of these strategies can be used in practicing five specific techniques for analyzing case studies: pattern matching, explanation building, time-series analysis, logic models, and cross-case synthesis. The first four are applicable whether a study involves a single- or a multiple-case design, and every case study should consider these techniques. Regardless of the choice of strategies or techniques, a persistent challenge is to produce high-quality analyses, which require investigators to attend to *all* the evidence, display and present the evidence separate from any interpretation, and show adequate concern for exploring alternative interpretations.

AN ANALYTIC STRATEGY: MORE THAN FAMILIARITY WITH ANALYTIC TOOLS

Need for an Analytic Strategy

The analysis of case study evidence is one of the least developed and most difficult aspects of doing case studies. Too many times, investigators start case studies without having the foggiest notion about how the evidence is to be analyzed (despite Chapter 3's recommendation that the analytic approaches be developed as part of the case study protocol). Such investigations easily become stalled at the analytic stage; this author has known colleagues who have simply ignored their case study data for month after month, not knowing what to do with the evidence.

Because of the problem, the experienced case study investigator is likely to have great advantages over the novice at the analytic stage. Unlike statistical analysis, there are few fixed formulas or cookbook recipes to guide the novice (one of the few texts providing useful advice is Miles & Huberman, 1994). Instead, much depends on an investigator's own style of rigorous thinking, along with the sufficient presentation of evidence and careful consideration of alternative interpretations.

At the same time, investigators and especially novices continue to be oriented toward the search for formulas, recipes, or *tools*, hoping that familiarity with these devices will produce the needed analytic result. The tools are important and can be useful, but they are usually most helpful if you know what to look for (i.e., have an overall analytic strategy), which returns you back to your original problem.

For instance, computer-assisted routines with prepackaged software, such as *n*onnumerical *u*nstructured *d*ata *i*ndexing, *s*earching, and *t*heorizing (NUD·IST) (e.g., Gahan & Hannibal, 1999) or Computer Assisted Qualitative Data Analysis Software (CAQDAS) (e.g., Fielding & Lee, 1998), have become increasingly used. The software helps you to code and categorize large amounts of narrative text, as might have been collected from open-ended interviews or from historic documents. Guidance on coding skills and techniques also has improved (e.g., Boyatzis, 1998; Strauss & Corbin, 1998).

The great benefit from such tools is when (a) the narrative texts represent a *verbatim* record of an interviewee's remarks or the literal content of a file or historic document, and (b) the empirical study is trying to derive meaning and insight from the word usage and frequency pattern found in the texts. (Indeed, *content analysis* was a pre-computer-age technique frequently used to analyze newspaper texts.) However, the verbatim or documentary records are likely to be only part of your total case study; alternatively, they may be the initial phase of a case study, aimed at surfacing salient concepts or themes (e.g., Strauss & Corbin, 1998). In either situation, you still need an analytic strategy to address the larger or fuller case study. (The main exception would be when your inquiry focused entirely on learning lessons from the verbatim or documentary text—but you should be aware that such a study would be a study of *verbal behavior* and not necessarily of actual events.)

Another set of helpful analytic manipulations has been comprehensively described and summarized by Miles and Huberman (1994) and includes

- Putting information into different arrays
- Making a matrix of categories and placing the evidence within such categories
- Creating data displays—flowcharts and other graphics—for examining the data
- Tabulating the frequency of different events
- Examining the complexity of such tabulations and their relationships by calculating second-order numbers such as means and variances
- Putting information in chronological order or using some other temporal scheme

These are indeed useful and important manipulations and can put the evidence in some preliminary order. Moreover, conducting such manipulations is one way of overcoming the stalling problem mentioned earlier. In this sense, manipulating the data at this early stage, or "playing with the data," can be a fruitful activity. Without a broader strategy, however, you are still likely to encounter many false starts and potentially waste large chunks of your time. Furthermore, if after playing with the data a general strategy does not emerge (or if you are not facile in playing with the data to begin with), the entire case study analysis is likely to be in jeopardy.

In a similar mode, yet another investigator has espoused the coding of case study events into numerical form, to make the case study data conducive to statistical analysis (Pelz, 1981). Such "quantitative" case studies may be possible when you have an embedded unit of analysis within a case study, but the approach still fails to address the need for doing analysis at the level of the whole case, where there may be only a single or a few cases—far too few for quantification to be helpful.

A higher priority than sheer familiarity with these tools and manipulations is to have a general analytic strategy in the first place. Once you have a strategy, the tools may turn out to be extremely useful (or irrelevant). The strategy will help you to treat the evidence fairly, produce compelling analytic conclusions, and rule out alternative interpretations. The strategy also will help you to use tools and make manipulations more effectively and efficiently. Three such strategies are described below, after which five specific techniques for analyzing case study data are reviewed. A continued alert is to be aware of these choices *before* collecting your data, so that you can be sure your data will be analyzable.

Three General Strategies

Relying on theoretical propositions. The first and most preferred strategy is to follow the theoretical propositions that led to your case study. The original objectives and design of the case study presumably were based on such propositions, which in turn reflected a set of research questions, reviews of the literature, and new hypotheses or propositions.

The propositions would have shaped your data collection plan and therefore would have given priorities to the relevant analytic strategies. One example, from a study of intergovernmental relationships, followed the proposition that federal funds not only have redistributive dollar effects but also create new organizational changes at the local level (Yin, 1980). The basic proposition—the creation of a "counterpart" bureaucracy in the form of local planning organizations, citizen action groups, and other new offices within a local government itself, but all attuned to specific federal programs—was traced in case studies of several cities. For each city, the purpose of the case study was to show how the formation and modification in local organizations occurred *after* changes in related federal programs, as well as how these local organizations acted on behalf of the federal programs even though they might have been components of local government.

This proposition is an example of a theoretical orientation guiding the case study analysis. Clearly, the proposition helps to focus attention on certain data and to ignore other data. (A good test is to decide what data you might cite if you had only 5 minutes to defend a proposition in your case study.) The proposition also helps to organize the entire case study and to define alternative explanations to be examined. Theoretical propositions about causal relations—answers to "how" and "why" questions—can be extremely useful in guiding case study analysis in this manner.

Thinking about rival explanations. A second general analytic strategy tries to define and test rival explanations. This strategy can be related to the first, in that the original theoretical propositions might have included rival hypotheses. However, the strategy is relevant even in the absence of such theoretical propositions and is especially useful in doing case study evaluations.

For instance, the typical hypothesis in an evaluation is that the observed outcomes were the result of an intervention supported by public or foundation funds. The simple or direct rival explanation would be that the observed outcomes were in fact the result of some other influence besides the intervention and that the investment of funds may not actually have been needed. Being aware (ahead of time) of this direct rival, your case study data collection should then have included attempts to collect evidence about the possible "other influences." Furthermore, you should have pursued your data collection about them vigorously—as if you were in fact trying to prove the salience of the other influences; then, if you had found

Type of Rival	Description or Examples
Craft Rivals:	
1. The Null Hypothesis	The observation is the result of chance circumstances only
2. Threats to Validity	e.g., history, maturation, instability, testing, instrumentation, regression, selection, experimental mortality, and selection-maturation interaction
3. Investigator Bias	e.g., "experimenter effect"; reactivity in field research
Real-Life Rivals:	
4. Direct Rival (Practice or Policy)	An intervention ("suspect 2") other than the target intervention ("suspect 1") accounts for the results ("the butler did it")
5. Commingled Rival (Practice or Policy)	Other interventions and the target intervention both contributed to the results ("it wasn't only me")
6. Implementation Rival	The implementation process, not the substantive intervention, accounts for the results ("did we do it right?")
7. Rival Theory	A theory different from the original theory explains the results better ("it's elementary, my dear Watson")
8. Super Rival	A force larger than but including the intervention accounts for the results ("it's bigger than both of us")
9. Societal Rival	Social trends, not any particular force or intervention, account for the results ("the times they are a-changin'")

Figure 5.1   Brief Descriptions of Different Kinds of Rival Explanations
SOURCE: Yin (2000).

insufficient evidence, you would less likely be accused of "stacking the deck" in favor of the original hypothesis (Patton, 1990, p. 462).

The direct rival—that the original investment was not the reason for the observed outcomes—is but one of several types of rival explanations. Figure 5.1 classifies and itemizes many types of rivals (Yin, 2000). For each type, an informal and more understandable descriptor accompanies the formal social science categorization, hoping to make the gist of the rival clearer.

The list reminds us of three "craft" rivals that underlie all of our social science research, and textbooks have given much attention to these craft rivals. However, the list also defines six "real-life" rivals that have received virtually no attention by other textbooks (nor, unfortunately, do most texts discuss the challenges and benefits of rival thinking or the use of rival explanations). These real-life rivals are the ones that you should carefully identify prior to your data collection (while not ignoring the craft rivals). Some real-life rivals also may not become apparent until you are in the midst of your data collection, and attending to them at that point is not only acceptable but also desirable. Overall, the more rivals that your analysis addresses and rejects, the more confidence you can place in your findings.

Rival explanations were a critical part of several of the case studies already contained in the BOXES cited earlier (e.g., refer to BOXES 1 and 11). The authors of these case studies used the rivals to drive their entire case study analysis. Additional examples of the use of rival explanations in case studies are presented in the companion to this book (Yin, 2003).[1]

Developing a case description. A third general analytic strategy is to develop a descriptive framework for organizing the case study. This strategy is less preferable than the use of theoretical propositions or rival explanations but serves as an alternative when you are having difficulty making either of the other approaches work.

Sometimes, the original purpose of the case study may have been a descriptive one. This was the objective of the famous sociological study *Middletown* (Lynd & Lynd, 1929), which was a case study of a small midwestern city. What is interesting about *Middletown,* aside from its classic value as a rich and historic case, is its structure, reflected by its chapters:

- Chapter I: Getting a Living
- Chapter II: Making a Home
- Chapter III: Training the Young
- Chapter IV: Using Leisure
- Chapter V: Engaging in Religious Practices
- Chapter VI: Engaging in Community Activities

These chapters cover a range of topics relevant to community life in the early 20th century, when Middletown was studied. The descriptive framework also organizes the case study analysis. (As an aside, a useful exercise is to note the structure of existing case studies—e.g., those cited in the BOXES throughout this book—and to examine their tables of contents, as an implicit clue to different analytic approaches.)

In other situations, the original objective of the case study may not have been a descriptive one, but a descriptive approach may help to identify the appropriate causal links to be analyzed—even quantitatively. BOX 24 gives an example of a case study that was concerned with the complexity of implementing a local public works program in Oakland, California. Such complexity, the investigators realized, could be *described* in terms of the multiplicity of decisions that had to occur for implementation to succeed. This descriptive insight later led to the enumeration, tabulation, and hence quantification of the various decisions. In this sense, the descriptive approach was used to identify (a) an embedded unit of analysis (see

---

BOX 24

Quantifying the Descriptive Elements of a Case Study

Pressman and Wildavsky's (1973) book, *Implementation: How Great Expectations in Washington Are Dashed in Oakland,* is regarded as one of the foremost contributions to the study of implementation (Yin, 1982b). This is the process whereby some programmatic activity—an economic development project, a new curriculum in a school, or a crime prevention program, for example—is installed in a specific setting (e.g., organization or community). The process is complex and involves numerous individuals, organizational rules, social norms, and mixtures of good and bad intentions.

Can such a complex process also be the subject of quantitative inquiry and analysis? Pressman and Wildavsky offer one innovative solution. To the extent that successful implementation can be *described* as a sequence of decisions, an analyst can focus part of the case study on the number and types of such decisions or elements.

Thus, in their chapter titled "The Complexity of Joint Action," the authors analyze the difficulties in Oakland: To implement one public works program required a total of 70 sequential decisions—project approvals, negotiation of leases, letting of contracts, and so on. The analysis examined the level of agreement and the time needed to reach agreement at each of the 70 decision points. Given the normal diversity of opinion and slippage in time, the analysis illustrates—in a quantitative manner—the low probability of implementation success.

Chapter 2) and (b) an overall pattern of complexity that ultimately was used in a causal sense to "explain" why implementation had failed.

Summary. The best preparation for conducting case study analysis is to have a general analytic strategy. Three have been described, relying on theoretical propositions, rival explanations, and case descriptions. These three general strategies underlie the specific analytic techniques to be described below. Without such strategies (or alternatives to them), case study analysis will proceed with difficulty.

The remainder of this chapter covers specific analytic techniques to be used as part of and along with any of the general strategies. The techniques are especially intended to deal with the previously noted problems of developing *internal validity* and *external validity* in doing case studies (see Chapter 2).

SPECIFIC ANALYTIC TECHNIQUES

None of the analytic techniques should be considered easy to use, and all will need much practice to be used powerfully. Your objective should be to start modestly, work thoroughly and introspectively, and build your own analytic repertoire over time. The reward will eventually emerge in the form of compelling case study analyses and, ultimately, compelling case studies.

Pattern Matching

For case study analysis, one of the most desirable techniques is using a pattern-matching logic. Such a logic (Trochim, 1989) compares an empirically based pattern with a predicted one (or with several alternative predictions). If the patterns coincide, the results can help a case study to strengthen its *internal validity*.

If the case study is an explanatory one, the patterns may be related to the dependent or the independent variables of study (or both). If the case study is a descriptive one, pattern matching is still relevant, as long as the predicted pattern of specific variables is defined prior to data collection.

Nonequivalent dependent variables as a pattern. The dependent-variables pattern may be derived from one of the more potent quasi-experimental research designs, labeled a "nonequivalent, dependent variables design" (Cook & Campbell, 1979, p. 118). According to this design, an experiment or quasi-experiment may have multiple dependent variables—that is, a variety of outcomes. If, for each outcome, the initially predicted values have been found, and at the same time alternative "patterns" of predicted values (including those deriving from methodological artifacts, or "threats" to validity) have not been found, strong causal inferences can be made.

For example, consider a single case in which you are studying the effects of a newly decentralized office computer system. Your major proposition is that—because each peripheral piece of equipment can work independently of any server—a certain pattern of organizational changes and stresses will be produced. Among these changes and stresses, you specify the following, based on propositions derived from previous decentralization theory:

- employees will create *new applications* for the office system, and these applications will be idiosyncratic to each employee;
- traditional *supervisory links* will be threatened, as management control over work tasks and the use of central sources of information will be diminished;

- *organizational conflicts* will increase, due to the need to coordinate resources and services across the decentralized units; but, nevertheless,
- *productivity* will increase over the levels prior to the installation of the new system.

In this example, these four outcomes each represent different dependent variables, and you would assess each with different measures and instruments. To this extent, you have a study that has specified *nonequivalent* dependent variables. You also have predicted an overall pattern of outcomes covering each of these variables. If the results are as predicted, you can draw a solid conclusion about the effects of decentralization. However, if the results fail to show the entire pattern as predicted—that is, even if one variable does not behave as predicted—your initial proposition would have to be questioned.

This first case could then be augmented by a second one, in which another new office system had been installed, but of a centralized nature— that is, the equipment at all of the individual workstations had been networked. Now you would predict a different pattern of outcomes, using the same four dependent variables enumerated above. And now, if the results show that the decentralized system (Case 1) had actually produced the predicted pattern and that this first pattern was different from that predicted and produced by the centralized system (Case 2), you would be able to draw an even stronger conclusion about the effects of decentralization. In this situation, you have made a *theoretical replication* across cases. (In other situations, you might have sought a *literal replication* by identifying and studying two or more cases of decentralized systems.)

Finally, you might be aware of the existence of certain threats to the validity of this logic (see Cook & Campbell, 1979, for a full list of these threats). For example, a new corporate executive might have assumed office in Case 1, leaving room for a counterargument: that the apparent effects of decentralization were actually attributable to this executive's appointment and not to the newly installed office system. To deal with this threat, you would have to identify some subset of the initial dependent variables and show that the pattern would have been different (in Case 1) if the corporate executive had been the actual reason for the effects. If you only had a single-case study, this type of procedure would be essential; you would be using the same data to rule out arguments based on a potential threat to validity. Given the existence of a second case, as in our hypothetical example, you also could show that the argument about the corporate executive would not explain certain parts of the pattern found in Case 2 (in which the absence of the corporate executive should have been associated

---

BOX 25

Pattern Matching for Rival Explanations

A common policy problem is to understand the conditions under which new research findings can be made useful to society. Too often, people think that research serves only itself and does not meet practical needs.

This topic was the subject of several case studies in which a research project's results were known to have been used. The case studies investigated how and why this outcome had occurred, entertaining several rival explanations based on three prevailing models of research use: (a) a research, development, and diffusion model; (b) a problem-solving model; and (c) a social interaction model (COSMOS, 1984a). The events of each case were compared to those predicted by each model in a pattern-matching mode. For instance, the problem-solving model requires the prior existence of a problem, as a prelude to the initiation of a research project, but the condition is not recognized by the other two models. This is therefore an example of how different theoretical models can predict mutually exclusive events, facilitating effective comparisons.

For all of the cases that were studied ($N = 9$), the events turned out to match best a combination of the second and third models. The investigators had therefore used rival explanations to analyze the data within each case and a replication logic across cases.

---

with certain opposing outcomes). In essence, your goal is to identify all reasonable threats to validity and to conduct repeated comparisons, showing how such threats cannot account for the dual patterns in both of the hypothetical cases.

Rival explanations as patterns. The use of rival explanations, besides being a good general analytic strategy, also provides a good example of pattern matching for *in*dependent variables. In such a situation (for an example, see BOX 25), several cases may be known to have had a certain type of outcome, and your investigation has focused on how and why this outcome occurred in each case.

This analysis requires the development of rival theoretical propositions, articulated in operational terms. The desired characteristic of these rival explanations is that each involves a pattern of independent variables that is mutually exclusive: If one explanation is to be valid, the others cannot be. This means that the presence of certain independent variables (predicted by one explanation) precludes the presence of other independent variables (predicted by a rival explanation). The independent variables may involve several or many different types of characteristics or events, each assessed with different measures and instruments. The concern of the case study analysis, however, is with the overall pattern of results and the degree to which the observed pattern matches the predicted one.

This type of pattern matching of independent variables also can be done either with a single case or with multiple cases. With a single case, the successful matching of the pattern to one of the rival explanations would be evidence for concluding that this explanation was the correct one (and that the other explanations were incorrect). Again, even with a single case, threats to validity—basically constituting another group of rival explanations—should be identified and ruled out. In addition, if this identical result were also obtained over multiple cases, *literal replication* of the single cases would have been accomplished, and the cross-case results might be stated even more assertively. Then, if this same result also failed to occur in a second group of cases, due to predictably different circumstances, *theoretical replication* would have been accomplished, and the initial result would stand yet more robustly.

Simpler patterns. This same logic can be applied to simpler patterns, having a minimal variety of either dependent or independent variables. In the simplest case, in which there may be only two different dependent (or independent) variables, pattern matching is possible as long as a different pattern has been stipulated for these two variables.

The fewer the variables, of course, the more dramatic the different patterns will have to be to allow any comparisons of their differences. Nevertheless, there are some situations in which the simpler patterns are both relevant and compelling. The role of the general analytic strategy would be to determine the best ways of contrasting any differences as sharply as possible and to develop theoretically significant explanations for the different outcomes.

Precision of pattern matching. At this point in the state of the art, the actual pattern-matching procedure involves no precise comparisons. Whether one is predicting a pattern of nonequivalent dependent variables, a pattern based on rival explanations, or a simple pattern, the fundamental comparison between the predicted and the actual pattern may involve no quantitative or statistical criteria. (Available statistical techniques are likely to be irrelevant because none of the variables in the pattern will have a "variance," each essentially representing a single data point.) The most precise quantitative result will likely occur if the study had set preestablished benchmarks—for example, productivity will increase by 10%—and the value of the actual outcome was then compared to this benchmark.

Low levels of precision can allow for some interpretive discretion on the part of the investigator, who may be overly restrictive in claiming a pattern to have been violated or overly lenient in deciding that a pattern has been matched. You can make your case study stronger by developing more precise measures. In the absence of such precision, an important suggestion is to avoid postulating very subtle patterns, so that your pattern matching deals with gross matches or mismatches whose interpretation is less likely to be challenged.

Explanation Building

A second analytic technique is in fact a special type of pattern matching, but the procedure is more difficult and therefore deserves separate attention. Here, the goal is to analyze the case study data by building an explanation about the case.

As used in this chapter, the procedure is mainly relevant to explanatory case studies. A similar procedure, for exploratory case studies, has been commonly cited as part of a hypothesis-generating process (see Glaser & Strauss, 1967), but its goal is not to conclude a study but to develop ideas for further study.

Elements of explanations. To "explain" a phenomenon is to stipulate a presumed set of causal links about it. These causal links are similar to the independent variables in the previously described use of rival explanations. In most studies, the links may be complex and difficult to measure in any precise manner.

In most existing case studies, explanation building has occurred in narrative form. Because such narratives cannot be precise, the better case studies are the ones in which the explanations have reflected some theoretically significant propositions. For example, the causal links may reflect critical insights into public policy process or social science theory. The public policy propositions, if correct, can lead to recommendations for future policy actions (see BOX 26, part A, for an example); the social science propositions, if correct, can lead to major contributions to theory building (see BOX 26, part B, for an example).

Iterative nature of explanation building. The explanation-building process, for explanatory case studies, has not been well documented in

---

BOX 26

A. Explanation Building in Multiple-Case Studies

In a multiple-case study, one goal is to build a general explanation that fits each of the individual cases, even though the cases will vary in their details. The objective is analogous to multiple experiments.

Martha Derthick's (1972) *New Towns In-Town: Why a Federal Program Failed* is a book about a housing program under President Lyndon Johnson's administration. The federal government was to give its surplus land—located in choice inner-city areas—to local governments for housing developments. But after 4 years, little progress had been made at the seven sites—San Antonio, New Bedford (Massachusetts), San Francisco, Washington, D.C., Atlanta, Louisville, and Clinton Township (Michigan)—and the program was considered a failure.

Derthick's account first analyzes the events at each of the seven sites. Then, a general explanation—that the projects failed to generate sufficient local support—is found unsatisfactory because the condition was not dominant at all of the sites. According to Derthick, local support did exist, but "federal officials had nevertheless stated such ambitious objectives that some degree of failure was certain" (p. 91). As a result, Derthick builds a modified explanation and concludes that "the surplus lands program failed both because the federal government had limited influence at the local level and because it set impossibly high objectives" (p. 93).

B. Explanation Building in Multiple-Case Studies: An Example From Another Field

An analytic approach similar to Derthick's is used by Barrington Moore (1966) in his history titled *Social Origins of Dictatorship and Democracy.* The book serves as another illustration of explanation building in multiple-case studies, even though the cases are actually historical examples.

Moore's book covers the transformation from agrarian to industrial societies in six different countries—England, France, the United States, China, Japan, and India—and the general explanation of the role of the upper classes and the peasantry is a basic theme that emerges. The explanation represented a significant contribution to the field of history.

---

operational terms. However, the eventual explanation is likely to be a result of a series of iterations:

- Making an initial theoretical statement or an initial proposition about policy or social behavior

- Comparing the findings of *an initial case* against such a statement or proposition
- Revising the statement or proposition
- Comparing other details of the case against the revision
- Comparing the revision to the facts of *a second, third, or more cases*
- Repeating this process as many times as is needed

In this sense, the final explanation may not have been fully stipulated at the beginning of a study and therefore differs from the pattern-matching approaches previously described. Rather, the case study evidence is examined, theoretical positions are revised, and the evidence is examined once again from a new perspective, in this iterative mode.

The gradual building of an explanation is similar to the process of refining a set of ideas, in which an important aspect is again to entertain other *plausible or rival explanations.* As before, the objective is to show how these explanations cannot be built, given the actual set of case study events. If this approach is applied to multiple-case studies (as in BOX 27), the result of the explanation-building process also may lead to starting a cross-case analysis, not simply an analysis of each individual case.

Potential problems in explanation building. You should be forewarned that this approach to case study analysis is fraught with dangers. Much analytic insight is demanded of the explanation builder. As the iterative process progresses, for instance, an investigator may slowly begin to drift away from the original topic of interest. Constant reference to the original purpose of the inquiry and the possible alternative explanations may help to reduce this potential problem. Other safeguards have already been covered by Chapters 3 and 4—that is, the use of a case study protocol (indicating what data were to be collected), the establishment of a case study database for each case (formally storing the entire array of data that were collected, available for inspection by a third party), and the following of a chain of evidence.

Time-Series Analysis

A third analytic technique is to conduct a time-series analysis, directly analogous to the time-series analysis conducted in experiments and quasi-experiments. Such analysis can follow many intricate patterns, which have been the subject of several major textbooks in experimental and clinical psychology with *single cases* (e.g., see Kratochwill, 1978); the interested reader is referred to such works for further detailed guidance. The more intricate and precise the pattern, the more that the time-series analysis also will lay a firm foundation for the conclusions of the case study.

BOX 27

Empirical Cases With a Theoretical "Case"

A common way of using case studies is to present the empirical evidence from a set of cases to test a theoretical "case." For Kelling and Coles (1997), the theoretical case was that a successful police strategy—helping communities to claim control over public spaces through proactive, zero-tolerance prosecutions of disorderly and related conduct ("taking back the streets")— emerged in the 1980s, resulting in substantial and subsequent reductions in more serious crimes. The authors argue their "case" by presenting evidence from specific case studies of New York City, Baltimore, San Francisco, and Seattle.

Especially relevant to case studies is an intriguing methodological analysis of qualitative research by Louise Kidder (1981), who demonstrated that certain types of participant-observer studies followed time-series designs, unbeknownst to the original investigators. For example, one study was concerned with the course of events that led to marijuana use, the hypothesis being that a sequence or "time series" of at least three conditions was necessary (Becker, 1963): initially smoking marijuana, later feeling its effects, and subsequently enjoying those effects. If a person experienced only one or two of these three steps but not all three, the hypothesis was that regular marijuana use would not follow. This type of postanalysis, on Kidder's part, needs to be repeated in the future to help reveal such implicit analytic techniques.

Simple time series. Compared to the more general pattern-matching analysis, a time-series design can be much simpler in one sense: In time series, there may only be a single dependent or independent variable. In these circumstances, when a large number of data points are relevant and available, statistical tests can even be used to analyze the data (see Kratochwill, 1978).

However, the pattern can be more complicated in another sense because the appropriate starting or ending points for this single variable may not be clear. Despite this problem, the ability to trace changes over time is a major strength of case studies—which are not limited to cross-sectional or static assessments of a particular situation. If the events over time have been traced in detail and with precision, some type of time-series analysis always may be possible, even if the case study analysis involves some other techniques as well.

The essential logic underlying a time-series design is the match between a trend of data points compared to (a) a theoretically significant trend specified before the onset of the investigation versus (b) some rival trend, also specified earlier, versus (c) any other trend based on some artifact or threat to internal validity. Within the same single-case study, for instance, two different patterns of events may have been hypothesized over time. This is what Campbell (1969) did in his now-famous study of the Connecticut speed limit law (see also Chapter 2, Figure 2.1). One time-series pattern was based on the proposition that the new law (an "interruption" in the time series) had substantially reduced the number of fatalities, whereas the other time-series pattern was based on the proposition that no such effect had occurred. The examination of the actual data points—that is, the annual number of fatalities over a period of years—was then made to determine which of the proposed time series best matched the empirical evidence. Such comparison of "interrupted time series" within the same case can be applied to many different settings.

In doing a multiple-case study, the same logic can be used, with different time-series patterns postulated for different cases. For instance, a case study about economic development in cities may have postulated the reasons that manufacturing-based cities would have more negative employment trends than those of service-based cities. The pertinent outcome data might have consisted of annual employment figures over a limited period of time, such as 10 years. In the manufacturing-based cities, the data might have been examined for a declining employment trend, whereas in the service-based cities, they might have been examined for a rising employment trend. Similar analyses can be imagined with regard to the examination of crime trends over time within individual cities, changes in housing markets, trends in annual student achievement or test scores, and many other indicators.

Complex time series. The time-series designs can be more complex when the trends within a given case are postulated to be more complex. One can postulate, for instance, not merely rising or declining trends but some rise followed by some decline within the same case. This type of mixed pattern, across time, would be the beginning of a more complex time series. As always, the strength of the case study strategy would not merely be in assessing this type of time series but also in having developed a rich explanation for the complex pattern of outcomes and in comparing the explanation with the outcomes.

Even greater complexities arise in those instances in which a multiple set of variables—not just a single one—are relevant to a case study and in which each variable is predicted to have a different pattern over time. A study of neighborhood change often assumes this characteristic. Typical neighborhood change theories, for instance, suggest that different time lags exist in the turnover rates among (a) the residential population, (b) commercial vendors and merchants, (c) local service institutions such as churches and public services, and (d) the housing stock (e.g., Yin, 1982a). When a neighborhood is undergoing racial change, upgrading, or other types of common transitions, all of these turnover rates may have to be studied over a 10- or 20-year period. The resulting curves, according to neighborhood change theories, will vary in predictable ways. For example, certain population changes (such as a subtle shift from small to larger families) are said to be followed first by certain changes in municipal services (such as school enrollment, as well as increases in the need for street services) but only later by turnover in commercial stores; furthermore, the types of churches may not change at all throughout this process.

Such a study frequently requires the collection of neighborhood indicators that in themselves are difficult to obtain, much less to analyze. However, if adequate time and effort have been set aside to conduct the necessary data collection and analysis, the result may be a compelling analysis—as in one study in which an "interrupted time-series design" was used to examine the long-term community effects of natural hazards. In this latter study, extensive data collection efforts were made in each of four communities, just to obtain the needed time-series data; the multiple-case results are described in BOX 28.

In general, although a more complex time-series creates greater problems for data collection, it also leads to a more elaborate trend (or set of trends) that can strengthen the analysis. Any match of a predicted with an actual time series, when both are complex, will produce strong evidence for an initial theoretical proposition.

Chronologies. The compiling of chronological events is a frequent technique in case studies and may be considered a special form of time-series analysis. The chronological sequence again focuses directly on the major strength of case studies cited earlier—that case studies allow you to trace events over time.

You should not think of the arraying of events into a chronology as a descriptive device only. The procedure can have an important analytic purpose—to investigate presumed causal events—because the basic sequence of a cause and its effect cannot be temporally inverted. Moreover, the

---

BOX 28

Case Studies Using Complex Time-Series Analyses

A natural disaster—such as a hurricane, tornado, or flood—can be considered a major disruptive event for a community. Sales and business patterns, crimes, and other population trends might all be expected to change as a result of such a disaster.

Paul Friesema and his colleagues (1979) studied such changes in four communities that had suffered from major disasters: Yuba City, California, 1955; Galveston, Texas, 1961; Conway, Arkansas, 1965; and Topeka, Kansas, 1966. In each of these case studies, the investigators collected extensive time-series data for various economic and social indicators. Their analysis showed that the disastrous event, though having a short-term effect—that is, within a 12-month period—had few, if any, long-term effects. This analysis represents an excellent application of a complex time-series technique as the basis for a multiple-case study.

---

chronology is likely to cover many different types of variables and not be limited to a single independent or dependent variable. In this sense, the chronology can be richer and more insightful than general time-series approaches. The analytic goal is to compare the chronology with that predicted by some explanatory theory—in which the theory has specified one or more of the following kinds of conditions:

- Some events must always occur before other events, with the reverse *sequence* being impossible.
- Some events must always be followed by other events, on a *contingency* basis.
- Some events can only follow other events after a prespecified *interval of time.*
- Certain *time periods* in a case study may be marked by classes of events that differ substantially from those of other time periods.

If the actual events of a case study, as carefully documented and determined by an investigator, have followed one predicted sequence of events and not those of a compelling rival sequence, the single-case study can again become the initial basis for causal inferences. Comparison to other cases, as well as the explicit consideration of threats to internal validity, will further strengthen this inference.

Summary conditions for time-series analysis. Whatever the stipulated nature of the time series, the important case study objective is to examine some relevant "how" and "why" questions about the relationship of events over time, not merely to observe the time trends alone. An interruption in a time series will be the occasion for postulating potential causal relationships; similarly, a chronological sequence should contain causal postulates.

On those occasions when the use of time-series analysis is relevant to a case study, an essential feature is to identify the specific indicator(s) to be traced over time, as well as the specific time intervals to be covered and the presumed temporal relationships among multiple events, stated by you prior to collecting the actual data. Only as a result of such prior specification are the relevant data likely to be collected in the first place, much less analyzed properly.

In contrast, if a study is limited to the analysis of time trends alone, as in a descriptive mode in which causal inferences are unimportant, a non–case study strategy is probably more relevant—for example, the economic analysis of consumer price trends over time.

Note, too, that without any hypotheses or causal propositions, chronologies become *chronicles*—valuable descriptive renditions of events but having no focus on causal inferences.

Logic Models

This fourth technique has become increasingly useful in recent years, especially in doing case study evaluations. The logic model deliberately stipulates a complex chain of events over time. The events are staged in repeated cause-effect-cause-effect patterns, whereby a dependent variable (event) at an earlier stage becomes the independent variable (causal event) for the next stage (Peterson & Bickman, 1992; Rog & Huebner, 1992). The complexity arises from the fact that multiple stages may exist over an extended period of time.

The use of logic models as an analytic technique consists of matching empirically observed events to theoretically predicted events. Conceptually, you therefore may consider the logic model technique to be another form of pattern matching. However, because of their sequential stages, logic models deserve to be distinguished as a separate analytic technique from pattern matching.

Joseph Wholey (1979) was at the forefront in developing logic models as an analytic technique. He first promoted the idea of a "program" logic model, tracing events when a public program intervention was intended to produce a certain outcome or sequence of outcomes. The *intervention* could initially produce activities with their own *immediate* outcomes; these immediate outcomes could, in turn, produce some *intermediate* outcomes; and, in turn, the intermediate outcomes were supposed to produce final or *ultimate* outcomes.

To illustrate Wholey's (1979) framework with a hypothetical example, a school *intervention* could have been organized to improve students' performance in high-stakes accountability tests now prevalent in K-12 education. The hypothetical intervention might have led to a new set of classroom activities during an extra hour in the school day. These activities would have provided time for students to work with their parents on joint exercises (*immediate outcome*). The result of this immediate outcome would have been a report of increased understanding and satisfaction with the educational process on the part of students, parents, and teachers (*intermediate outcome*). Eventually, the exercises and the satisfaction would have led to increased learning of certain concepts by students (*ultimate outcome*).

In this example, the case study analysis would organize the empirical data to support (or to challenge) this logic model. Going beyond Wholey's (1979) approach and using the strategy of rival explanations espoused earlier in this book, the analysis also would entertain rival chains of events, as well as the potential importance of spurious external events. If the data were supportive of the initial chain, and no rivals could be substantiated, the analysis could claim a causal effect between the initial school intervention and the later increased learning. Alternatively, the conclusion might be reached that the specified series of events was *illogical*—for instance, that the school intervention had involved students at a different grade level than whose learning had been assessed.

The program logic model strategy can be used in a variety of circumstances, not just those in which a public policy intervention has occurred. A key ingredient is the claimed existence of repeated cause-and-effect sequences of events, all linked together. The more complex the link, the more definitively the case study data can be analyzed to determine whether a pattern match has been made with these events over time. Four types of logic models are discussed next. They mainly vary according to the *unit of analysis* that might be relevant to your case study.

Individual-level logic model. The first type assumes that your case study is about an individual person, with Figure 5.2 depicting the behavioral course of events for a hypothetical youth. The events flow across a series of boxes and arrows reading from left to right in the figure. It suggests that the youth may be at risk for becoming a member of a gang, may eventually become involved in gang violence and drugs, and later may even be part of a gang-related criminal offense. Distinctive about this logic model is the series of 11 numbers associated with the various arrows in the figure. Each of the 11 represents an opportunity, through some type of planned

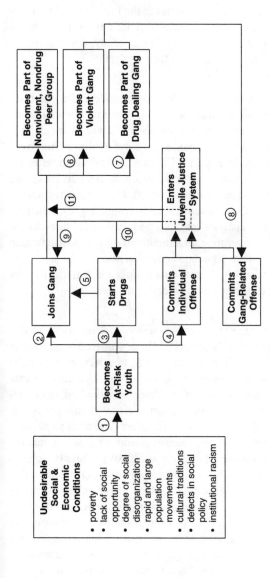

Figure 5.2 Youth Behavior and 11 Possible Interventions
SOURCE: COSMOS Corporation.

① = Community and social strategies are aimed at disrupting this path
②, ③, ④ = Prevention strategies are aimed at disrupting these paths
⑤ = Drug treatment interdiction strategies are aimed at disrupting this path
⑥, ⑦, ⑧ = Law enforcement interdiction and suppression are aimed at disrupting these paths
⑨, ⑩ = Early intervention, justice system strategies are aimed at disrupting these paths
⑪ = Justice system interdiction strategies are aimed at disrupting this path

intervention (e.g., community or public program), to prevent an individual youth from continuing on the flow. For instance, community development programs (number 1) might improve the social and economic conditions to reduce the youth's chances of becoming at risk in the first place. How a particular youth might have encountered and dealt with any or all of the 11 possible interventions might be the subject of a case study, with Figure 5.2 helping you to define the relevant data and their analysis.

Firm or organizational-level logic model. Logic models also can trace events taking place in an individual organization, such as a manufacturing firm. Figure 5.3 shows how changes in a firm (boxes 5 and 6) are claimed to lead to improved manufacturing (box 8) and eventually to improved business performance (boxes 10 and 11). The flow of boxes also reflects a hypothesis—that the initial changes were the result of external brokerage and technical assistance services (boxes 2 and 3). Given this hypothesis, the logic model therefore also contains rival or competing explanations (boxes 12 and 13). The data analysis for this case study would then consist of tracing the actual events over time, at a minimum giving close attention to their chronological sequence. The data collection also should have tried to identify ways in which the boxes were actually linked in real life, thereby corroborating the layout of the arrows connecting the boxes.

An alternative configuration for an organizational-level logic model. Graphically, nearly all logic models construe a linear sequence (e.g., reading from left to right or from top to bottom). In real life, however, events can be more dynamic, not necessarily progressing linearly. One such set of events might occur in relation to the "reforming" or "transformation" of an organization. For instance, business firms may undergo many significant operational changes, and the business's mission and culture (and even name) also may change. The significance of these changes warrants the notion that the entire business has been transformed (COSMOS, 2000).[2] Similarly, schools or school systems can sufficiently alter their way of doing business that "systemic reform" is said to be occurring. In fact, major public initiatives deliberately aim at improving schools by encouraging the reform of entire school systems (i.e., school districts). However, neither the transformation nor reform processes are linear in at least two ways. First, changes may reverse course and not just progress in one direction. Second, the completed transformation or systemic reform is not necessarily an end point implied by the linear logic model (i.e., the final box in the model); continued transform*ing* and reform*ing* may be ongoing processes even over the long haul.

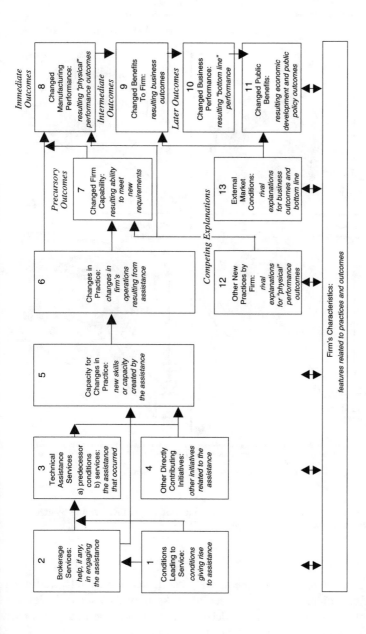

Figure 5.3 Changes in Performance in a Manufacturing Firm
SOURCE: Yin and Oldsman (1995).

Key: A = Assessment; C = Standards-Based Curriculum; DP = District Policies; EQ = Equity; PS = Preservice Requirements; PD = Professional Development; R = Resource Convergence; S = Stakeholder Support and Partnerships; SP = State Policies; T = Technology; TC = Teacher Certification Requirements;

Scale up in Schools and Classrooms = Few or none ●   Some   🚩   Large majority 🚩🚩

Figure 5.4 Hypothetical States of an Education (K–12) Reforming System
SOURCE: COSMOS Corporation (2001).

Figure 5.4 presents an alternatively configured logic model, reflecting these conditions. This logic model (a) tracks all of the main activities in a school system (the initials are decoded in the key to the figure), (b) over four periods of time (each time interval might represent a 2- or 3-year period of time). Systemic reform occurs when all of the activities are aligned and work together, and this occurs at t_3 in Figure 5.4. At later stages, however, the reform may regress, represented by t_4, and the logic model does not assume that the vacillations will even end at t_4. As a further feature of the logic model, the entire circle at each stage can be positioned higher or lower, representing the level of student performance—the hypothesis being that systemic reform will be associated with the highest performance. The pennants in the middle of the circle indicate the number of schools or classrooms implementing the desired reform practices, and this number also can vacillate. Finally, the logic model contains a "metric," whereby the positioning of the activities or the height of the circle can be defined as a result of analyzing actual data.

Program-level logic model. Returning to the more conventional linear model, Figure 5.5 contains a fourth and final example. Here, the model depicts the rationale underlying a major federal program, aimed at reducing the incidence of HIV/AIDS by supporting community planning and prevention initiatives. The program provides funds as well as technical assistance to 65 state and local health departments across the United States. The model was used to organize and analyze data from 14 case studies (COSMOS, 1999), including the collection of data on rival explanations, whose potential role also is shown in the model.

Summary. Using logic models represents a fourth technique for analyzing case study data. Four types of logic models, applying to different units of analysis and situations, have been presented. You should define your logic model prior to collecting data and then "test" the model by seeing how well the data support it.[3]

Cross-Case Synthesis

A fifth technique applies specifically to the analysis of multiple cases (the previous four techniques can be used with either single- or multiple-case studies). The technique is especially relevant if, as advised in Chapter 2, a case study consists of at least two cases. The analysis is likely to be easier and the findings likely to be more robust than having only a single case. BOX 29 presents an excellent example of the important research and research topics that can be addressed by having a "two-case" case study. Again, having more than two cases could strengthen the findings even further.

Cross-case syntheses can be performed whether the individual case studies have previously been conducted as independent research studies

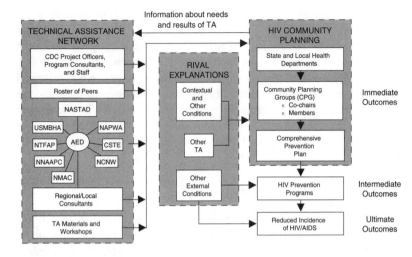

Figure 5.5   Improving Community Planning for HIV/AIDS Prevention
SOURCE: COSMOS Corporation (1999).

(authored by different persons) or as a predesigned part of the same study. In either situation, the technique treats each individual case study as a separate study. In this way, the technique does not differ from other research syntheses—aggregating findings across a series of individual studies (see BOX 30). If there are large numbers of individual case studies available, the synthesis can incorporate quantitative techniques common to other research syntheses (e.g., Cooper & Hedges, 1994) or meta-analyses (e.g., Lipsey, 1992). However, if only a modest number of case studies is available, alternative tactics are needed.

One possibility is to create word tables that display the data from the individual cases according to some uniform framework. Figure 5.6 has an example of such a word table, capturing the findings from 14 case studies of organizational centers, with each center having an organizational partner (COSMOS, 1998). Of the 14 centers, 7 had received programmatic support and were considered intervention centers; the other 7 were selected as comparison centers. For both types of centers, data were collected about the center's ability to colocate (e.g., share facilities) with its partnering organization—this being only one of several outcomes of interest in the original study.

The overall pattern in the word table led to the conclusion that the intervention and comparison centers did not differ with regard to this particular

---

BOX 29

**Using a "Two-Case" Case Study to Test
a Policy-Oriented Theory**

The international marketplace of the 1970s and 1980s was marked by Japan's prominence. Much of its strength was attributable to the role of centralized planning and support by a special governmental ministry— considered by many to be an unfair competitive edge, compared to the policies in other countries. For instance, the United States was considered to have no counterpart support structures. Gregory Hooks's (1990) excellent case study points to a counterexample, frequently ignored by advocates: the role of the U.S. Department of Defense in implementing an industrial planning policy within defense-related industries.

Hooks provides quantitative data on two cases—the aeronautics industry and the microelectronics industry (the forerunner to the entire computer chip market and its technologies, such as the personal computer). One industry (aeronautics) has traditionally been known to be dependent on support from the federal government, but the other has not. In both cases, Hooks's evidence shows how the defense department supported the critical early development of these industries through financial support, the support of R&D, and the creation of an initial customer base for the industry's products. The existence of both cases, and not the aeronautics industry alone, makes the author's entire argument powerful and persuasive.

---

outcome. Additional word tables, reflecting other processes and outcomes of interest, were examined in the same way. The analysis of the entire collection of word tables enabled the study to draw cross-case conclusions about the intervention centers and their outcomes.

Complementary word tables can go beyond the single features of a case and array a whole set of features on a case-by-case basis. Now, the analysis can start to probe whether different groups of cases appear to share some similarity and deserve to be considered instances of the same "type" of general case. Such an observation can further lead to analyzing whether the arrayed case studies reflect subgroups or categories of general cases—raising the possibility of a typology of individual cases that can be highly insightful. This illustrative example shows how cross-case syntheses can become more complex and cover broader issues than simply analyzing single features.

An important caveat in conducting this kind of cross-case synthesis is that the examination of word tables for cross-case patterns will rely

---

BOX 30

Eleven Program Evaluations and a Cross-"Case" Analysis

Dennis Rosenbaum (1986) collected 11 program evaluations as separate chapters in an edited book. The 11 evaluations had been conducted by different investigators, had used a variety of methods, and were not case studies. Each evaluation was about a different community crime prevention intervention, and some presented ample quantitative evidence and employed statistical analyses. The evaluations were deliberately selected because nearly all had shown positive results. A cross-"case" analysis was conducted by the present author (Yin, 1986), treating each evaluation as if it were a separate "case." The analysis dissected and arrayed the evidence from the 11 evaluations in the form of word tables. Generalizations about successful community crime prevention, independent of any specific intervention, were then derived by using a replication logic, given that all of the evaluations had shown positive results.

Centers	Characteristics of Co-Location
Intervention Centers:	
1	Partnering staff are located in the same facility as Center 1 and follow Center 1's policies that were in place prior to the partnership. Center 1 receives $25,000 annually from the partnership budget for software and peripherals, and communication and supplies.
2	As a business unit of Center 2, the partnering staff are housed within Center 2's offices. Center 2's parent organization contributes $2,500 for space and $23,375 for indirect expenses annually to the partnership budget.
3	Five partnership offices are co-located with Center 3's staff.
4	Center 4 and its partner share office space.
5	Center 5 staff and the partnering staff are located in the same building, but do not share office space.
6	The two organizations are not co-located.
7	Partnering staff are located in Center 7's offices.
Comparison Centers:	
8	Center 8 and its partner share office space in eight locations statewide.
9	Some sites are co-located.
10	Center 10 and its partner are not co-located.
11	The partnering and center staff share office space.
12	Center 12 and its partner's staff are located in the same building.
13	Center 13 and its partner's staff are located in the same office.
14	Center 14 shares office space with three regional partners.

Figure 5.6   Co-location of Interorganizational Partners (14 Centers and Their Counterpart Organizations)
SOURCE: COSMOS Corporation (1998).

strongly on argumentative interpretation, not numeric tallies. Chapter 2 has previously pointed out, however, that this method is directly analogous to cross-*experiment* interpretations, which also have no numeric properties when only a small number of experiments is available for analysis. A challenge you must be prepared to meet as a case study investigator is therefore to know how to develop strong, plausible, and fair arguments that are supported by the data.

PRESSING FOR A HIGH-QUALITY ANALYSIS

No matter what specific analytic strategy or techniques have been chosen, you must do everything to make sure that your analysis is of the highest quality. At least four principles underlie all good social science research (Yin, 1994a, 1997, 1999) and require your attention.

First, your analysis should show that you attended to *all the evidence.* Your analytic strategies, including the development of rival hypotheses, must be exhaustive. Your analysis should show how it sought as much relevant evidence as was available, and your interpretations should account for all of this evidence and leave no loose ends. Without achieving this standard, your analysis may be vulnerable to alternative interpretations based on the evidence that you had (inadvertently) ignored.

Second, your analysis should address, if possible, *all major rival interpretations.* If someone else has an alternative explanation for one or more of your findings, make this alternative into a rival. Is there evidence to address this rival? If so, what are the results? If not, should the rival be restated as a loose end to be investigated in future studies?

Third, your analysis should address *the most significant aspect* of your case study. Whether it is a single- or multiple-case study, you will have demonstrated your best analytic skills if the analysis focuses on the most important issue (preferably defined at the outset of the case study). In addition, by avoiding a detour to a lesser issue, your analysis will be less vulnerable to the possibility that the main issue was being avoided because of possibly negative findings.

Fourth, you should use your own *prior, expert knowledge* in your case study. The strong preference here is for you to demonstrate awareness of current thinking and discourse about the case study topic. If you know your subject matter as a result of your own previous investigations and publications, so much the better.

The case study in BOX 31 was done by a research team with academic credentials and strong practical experience. By taking several steps, the

---

BOX 31

**Analytic Quality in a Multiple-Case Study
of International Trade Competition**

The quality of a case study analysis is not dependent solely on the techniques used, although they are important. Equally important is that the investigator demonstrate expertise in carrying out the analysis. This expertise was reflected in Magaziner and Patinkin's (1989) book, *The Silent War: Inside the Global Business Battles Shaping America's Future.*

The authors organized their nine cases in excellent fashion. Across cases, major themes regarding America's competitive advantages (and disadvantages) were covered in a replication design. Within each case, the authors provided extensive interview and other documentation, showing the sources of their findings. (To keep the narrative reading smoothly, much of the data—in word tables, notes, and quantitative tabulations—were relegated to footnotes and appendices.) In addition, the authors showed that they had extensive personal exposure to the issues being studied as a result of numerous domestic and overseas visits.

Technically, a more explicit methodological section might have been helpful. However, the careful and detailed work, even in the absence of such a section, helps to illustrate what all investigators should strive to achieve.

---

authors demonstrate a care of empirical investigation whose spirit is worth considering in all case studies. The care is reflected in the presentation of the cases themselves, not by the existence of a stringent methodology section. If you can emulate these and other strategies in your analysis, your case study analysis also will be given appropriate respect and recognition.

SUMMARY

This chapter has presented several ways of analyzing case studies. First, the potential analytic difficulties can be reduced if you have a general strategy for analyzing the data—whether such a strategy is based on theoretical propositions, rival explanations, or descriptive frameworks. In the absence of such strategies, you may have to "play with the data" in a preliminary sense, as a prelude to developing a systematic sense of what is worth analyzing and how it should be analyzed.

Second, given a general strategy, several specific analytic techniques are relevant. Of these, five (pattern matching, explanation building, time-series analysis, logic models, and cross-case syntheses) can be effective in laying the groundwork for high-quality case studies. For all five, a similar replication logic should be applied if a study involves multiple cases (thereby gaining external validity). Comparisons to rival propositions and threats to internal validity also should be made within each individual case.

None of these techniques is easy to use. None can be applied mechanically, following any simple cookbook procedure. Not surprisingly, case study analysis is the most difficult stage of doing case studies, and novice investigators are especially likely to have a troublesome experience. Again, one recommendation is to begin with a simple and straightforward case study (or, more preferably, a "two-case" design), even if the research questions are not as sophisticated or innovative as might be desired. Experience gained in completing such straightforward case studies will lead to the ability to tackle more difficult topics in subsequent case studies.

EXERCISES

1. *Creating a general analytic strategy.* Assume you have collected your case study data but still do not have an analytic strategy. Ask yourself how you might organize your case into separate chapters or sections. Use substantive titles and headings (e.g., instead of "Introduction," make the title say what the introduction is about, even if more than a few words are needed). Try different sequences of titles, noting how such differences might also alter your analytic strategy. Now choose one sequence and start sorting your data into the designated chapters or sections. You should be on your way to analyzing your case study.

2. *Analyzing the analytic process.* Select one of the case studies described in the BOXES of this book. Find one of the chapters (usually in the middle of the study) in which evidence is presented but conclusions also are being made. Describe how this linkage—from cited evidence to conclusions—occurs. Are data displayed in tables or other formats? Are comparisons being made?

3. *Merging quantitative and qualitative data.* Name some topic within a case study you might be conducting for which both qualitative and quantitative data might be relevant. Identify the two types of data, assume they have been collected successfully, and discuss the ways in which they would be combined or compared. What is the value of having each type of data?

4. *Matching patterns.* Name a case study that used a pattern-matching technique in its analysis. What peculiar advantages and disadvantages does it have to offer? How can the technique produce a compelling analysis even when applied to only a single case?

5. *Constructing an explanation.* Identify some observable changes that have been occurring in your neighborhood (or the neighborhood around your campus). Develop an explanation for these changes and indicate the critical set of evidence you would collect to support or challenge this explanation. If such evidence were available, would your explanation be complete? Compelling? Useful for investigating similar changes in another neighborhood?

6. *Analyzing time-series trends.* Identify a simple time series—for example, the number of students enrolled in your university for each of the past 20 years. How would you compare one period of time with another within the 20-year period? If the university admissions policies had changed during this time, how would you compare the effects of such policies? How might this analysis be considered part of a broader case study of your university?

NOTES

1. See Chapters 4, 5, 8, and 10. The first two of these chapters summarize the cases by deliberately focusing on the rival explanation(s). The second two of these chapters contain complete case studies, showing how rival explanations were used as part of the case study analysis.

2. Chapter 10 of the companion book presents the full cross-case analysis of a study of transformed firms.

3. The companion book has many additional examples of the use of logic models in specific case studies. See Chapters 6, 8, and 10.

6

Reporting Case Studies

Reporting a case study means bringing its results and findings to closure. Regardless of the form of the report, similar steps underlie the case study composition: identifying the audience for the report, developing the compositional structure, and following certain procedures (such as having the report reviewed by informed persons who have been the subject of the case study). Once composed, the case study may be finished—or it may be joined with data collected through other methods as part of a broader, multimethod study. Such studies can be advantageous and represent a further challenge in doing case study research.

Whether serving as a finished case study or as part of a multi-method study, reporting case study results also is one of the most challenging aspects of doing case studies. The best general advice is to compose portions of the case study early (e.g., the bibliography and the methodology section), rather than waiting until the end of the data analysis process. As for compositional structures, six alternatives are suggested: linear-analytic, comparative, chronological, theory-building, "suspense," and unsequenced structures. A final plea is to worry about producing high-quality and not just run-of-the-mill case studies.

As a general rule, the compositional phase puts the greatest demands on a case study investigator. The case study report does not follow any stereotypic form, such as a journal article in psychology. Moreover, the report need not be in written form only; you may have the opportunity to make an oral presentation about your case study. Because of this uncertain nature, researchers who do not like to compose may want to question their interest in doing case studies in the first place.

Of course, most investigators can eventually learn to compose easily and well, and inexperience in composing should not be a deterrent to doing case studies. However, much practice will be needed. Furthermore, to do good case studies, you should want to become good at composing—and not merely put up with it. One indicator of whether you are likely to succeed at this phase of the craft is whether term papers were easy or difficult to do in high school or college. The more difficult they were, the more difficult it will be to compose a case study report. Another indicator is whether composing is viewed as an opportunity or as a burden. The successful investigator usually perceives the compositional phase as an opportunity—to make a significant contribution to knowledge or practice.

Unfortunately, few people are forewarned about this problem that lies at the end of designing and doing a case study. However, the smart investigator will begin to compose the case study report even before data collection and analysis have been completed. In general, the compositional phase is so important that you should give it explicit attention throughout the earlier phases of your case study.

Despite this advice, most investigators typically ignore the compositional phase until the very end of their case studies. Under these circumstances, all sorts of "writer's cramps" may appear, and the case study report may become impossible to compose. Thus, a prelude to any case study research may be to consult a textbook covering the writing of research reports more generally (e.g., Barzun & Graff, 1985; Becker, 1986). Such texts offer invaluable reminders for taking notes, making outlines, using plain words, writing clear sentences, establishing a schedule for composing, and combatting the common urge not to compose.

The purpose of this chapter is not to repeat these general lessons, although they are applicable to case studies. Most of the lessons are important to all forms of research composition, and to describe them here would defeat the purpose of providing information specific to case studies. Instead, the main purpose of this chapter is to highlight those aspects of composition and reporting that are directly related to case studies. These include the following topics, each covered in a separate section:

- Targeting case study reports
- Case study reports as part of larger multimethod studies
- Illustrative structures for case study compositions
- Procedures to be followed in doing a case study report
- And, in conclusion, speculations on the characteristics of an exemplary case study (extending beyond the report itself and covering the design and content of the case)

One reminder from Chapter 4 is that the case study report should not be the main way of recording or storing the evidentiary base of the case study. Rather, Chapter 4 advocated the use of a case study database for this purpose (see Chapter 4, Principle 2), and the compositional efforts described in this chapter are primarily intended to serve reporting and not documentation objectives.

TARGETING CASE STUDY REPORTS

Giving some initial thought to your likely or preferred audience and reporting formats serves as a good starting point for composing your case study. It can have a more diverse set of possible audiences than most other types of research, including (a) academic colleagues; (b) policymakers, practitioners, community leaders, and other professionals who do not specialize in case study or other social science research; (c) special groups such as a dissertation or thesis committee; and (d) funders of research.[1]

With most research reports, such as experiments, the second audience is not typically relevant, as few would expect the result of a laboratory experiment to be directed to nonspecialists. However, for case studies, this second audience may be a frequent target of the case study report. As another contrast, the third audience would rarely be relevant for some types of research—such as evaluations—because evaluations are not usually suitable as theses or dissertations. However, for case studies, this third audience also is a frequent consumer of the case study report due to the large number of theses and dissertations in the social sciences that rely on case studies.

Because case studies have more potential audiences than other types of research, one of your essential tasks in designing the overall case study report is to identify the specific audiences for the report. Each audience has different needs, and no single report will serve all audiences simultaneously.

As examples, for *academic colleagues,* the connections among the case study, its findings, and previous theory or research are likely to be most important (see BOX 32). For *nonspecialists,* the descriptive elements in portraying some real-life situation, as well as the implications for action, are likely to be more important. For a *thesis committee,* mastery of the methodology and theoretical issues, along with an indication of the care with which the research was conducted, is important. Finally, for *research funders,* the significance of the case study findings, whether cast in academic or practical terms, is probably as important as the rigor with which the research was conducted. Successful communication with more than one audience may mean the need for more than one version of a case study report. Investigators should seriously consider catering to such a need (see BOX 33).

BOX 32

Famous Case Study Reprinted

For many years, Philip Selznick's (1949/1980) *TVA and the Grass Roots* has stood as a classic about public organizations. The case has been cited in many subsequent studies of federal agencies, political behavior, and organizational decentralization.

Fully 30 years after its original publication, this case was reprinted in 1980 as part of the Library Reprint Series by the University of California Press, the original publisher. This type of reissuance allows numerous other researchers to have access to this famous case study and reflects its substantial contribution to the field.

BOX 33

Two Versions of the Same Case Study

The city planning office of Broward County, Florida, implemented an office automation system beginning in 1982 ("The Politics of Automating a Planning Office," Standerfer & Rider, 1983). The implementation strategies were innovative and significant—especially in relation to tensions with the county government's computer department. As a result, the case study is interesting and informative, and a popularized version—appearing in a practitioner journal—is fun and easy to read.

Because this type of implementation also covers complex technical issues, the authors made supplementary information available to the interested reader. The popularized version provided a name, address, and telephone number, so that such a reader could obtain the additional information. This type of dual availability of case study reports is but one example of how different reports of the *same* case study may be useful for communicating with different audiences.

Communicating With Case Studies

One additional difference between the case study and other types of research is that your case study report can itself be a significant communication device. For many nonspecialists, the description and analysis of a single case often suggest implications about a more general phenomenon.

A related situation, often overlooked, occurs with testimony before a congressional committee. If an elderly person, for instance, testifies about his or her health services before such a committee, its members may assume that they have acquired an understanding of health care for the elderly more generally—based on this "case." Only then might the members be willing to review broader statistics about the prevalence of similar cases. Later, the committee may inquire about the representative nature of the initial case before proposing new legislation. However, throughout this entire process, the initial "case"—represented by a witness—may have been the essential ingredient in calling attention to the health care issue in the first place.

In these and other ways, your case study can communicate research-based information about a phenomenon to a variety of nonspecialists. Your case study may even assume the form of a videotape or other multimedia device and not a narrative report (e.g., see Naumes & Naumes, 1999, chap. 10). The usefulness of case studies therefore goes far beyond the role of the typical research report, which is generally addressed to colleagues rather than nonspecialists (see BOX 34). Obviously, descriptive as well as explanatory case studies can be important in this role, and you should not overlook the potential descriptive impact of a well-presented case study.

Orienting the Case Study Report to an Audience's Needs

Overall, the preferences of the potential audience should dictate the form of your case study report. Although the research procedures and methodology should have followed other guidelines, suggested in Chapters 1 through 5, your report should reflect emphases, detail, compositional forms, and even a length suitable to the needs of the potential audience. The importance of the audience suggests that you might want to collect formal information about what the audiences need and their preferred types of communication (Morris, Fitz-Gibbon, & Freeman, 1987, p. 13). Along these lines, this author has frequently called the attention of thesis or dissertation students to the fact that the thesis or dissertation committee may be their *only* audience. The ultimate report, under these conditions, should attempt to communicate directly with this committee. A recommended tactic is to integrate the committee members' previous research into the thesis or dissertation, creating greater conceptual (and methodological) overlap and thereby increasing its potential communicability to that particular audience.

Whatever the audience, the greatest error you can make is to compose a report from an egocentric perspective. This error will occur if you complete

---

BOX 34

Making a Good Case Study Available to a Wider Audience

Neustadt and Fineberg's (1983) excellent analysis of a mass immunization campaign was issued originally as a government report in 1978, *The Swine Flu Affair: Decision-Making on a Slippery Disease.* This case study was thereafter cited, among public policy circles, as an example of a thorough and high-quality case study, and the case also was used frequently for teaching purposes.

The original form of the case study, however, was difficult to obtain, having been published by the U.S. Government Printing Office, which, according to the authors, "has many virtues, . . . but . . . filling orders which do not have exact change and precise stock numbers is not one of them" (Neustadt & Fineberg, 1983, p. xxiv). As a result, a revised version of the original case study—adding new material to the original case—was later published as *The Epidemic That Never Was* (1983). This commercial issuance of such a highly regarded case study is a rare example of what can be done to improve the dissemination of case studies.

---

your report without identifying a specific audience or without understanding the specific needs of such an audience. To avoid this error, one suggestion is to identify the audience, as previously noted. A second and equally important suggestion is to examine previous case study reports that have successfully communicated with this audience. Such prior reports may offer helpful clues for composing a new report. For instance, consider again the thesis or dissertation student. The student should consult previous dissertations and theses that have passed the academic regimen successfully—or are known to have been exemplary works. The inspection of such works may yield sound information regarding the departmental norms (and reviewers' likely preferences) for designing a new thesis or dissertation.

Formats for Written Case Study Reports

Among written forms of case studies, there are at least four important varieties. The first is the classic single-case study. A single narrative is used to describe and analyze the case. You may augment the narrative with tabular as well as graphic and pictorial displays. Depending on the depth of the case study, these classic single cases are likely to appear as books because journals cannot accommodate the needed space. As a word of

---

BOX 35

A Multiple-Case Report

Multiple-case studies often contain both the individual case studies and some cross-case chapters. The composition of such a multiple-case study also may be shared among several authors.

This type of arrangement was used in a study of eight innovations in mathematics and science education, edited by Raizen and Britton (1997). The study, titled *Bold Ventures,* appears in three separate and lengthy volumes (about 250, 350, and 650 pages, respectively). The individual case studies appear in the last two volumes, whereas the seven chapters in Volume 1 cover cross-case issues. Many different and multiple authors conducted both the individual case studies and the cross-case chapters, although the entire study was orchestrated and coordinated as a single undertaking.

---

advice, if you know ahead of time that your case study will fall into this category and that you can produce only a book-length manuscript, you should be establishing some early contact with a publisher.

A second type of written product is the multiple-case version of this classic single case. This type of multiple-case report will contain multiple narratives, usually presented as separate chapters or sections about each of the cases singly. In addition to these individual case narratives, your report also will contain a chapter or section covering the cross-case analysis and results. Some situations may even call for several cross-case chapters or sections, and the cross-case portion of the final text may justify a volume separate from the individual case narratives (see BOX 35). In these situations, a frequent form of presentation is to have the bulk of the main report contain the cross-case analysis, with the individual cases presented as part of a long appendix to that basic volume.

A third type of written product covers either a multiple- or a single-case study but does not contain the traditional narrative. Instead, the composition for each case follows a series of questions and answers, based on the questions and answers in the case study database (see Chapter 4). For reporting purposes, the content of the database is shortened and edited for readability, with the final product still assuming the format, analogously, of a comprehensive examination. (In contrast, the traditional case study narrative may be considered similar to the format of a term paper.) This question-and-answer format may not reflect your full creative talent, but the format helps to avoid the problems of writer's cramps. This is because you can proceed immediately to answer the required set of questions. (Again, the comprehensive exam has a similar advantage over a term paper.)

BOX 36

**A Question-and-Answer Format: Case Studies Without
the Traditional Narrative**

Case study evidence does not need to be presented in the traditional narrative form. An alternative format for presenting the same evidence is to write the narrative in question-and-answer form. A series of questions can be posed, with the answers taking some reasonable length—for example, three or four paragraphs each. Each answer can contain all the relevant evidence and can even be augmented with tabular presentations and citations.

This alternative was followed in 40 case studies of community organizations produced by the U.S. National Commission on Neighborhoods (1979), *People, Building Neighborhoods*. The same question-and-answer format was used in each case, so that the interested reader could do his or her own cross-case analysis by following the same question across all of the cases. The format allowed hurried readers to find exactly the relevant portions of each case. For people offended by the absence of the traditional narrative, each case also called for a summary, unconstrained in its form (but no longer than three pages), allowing the author to exercise his or her more literary talents.

If this question-and-answer format has been used for multiple-case studies, the advantages are potentially enormous: A reader need only examine the answers to the same question or questions within each case study to begin making cross-case comparisons. Because each reader may be interested in different questions, the entire format facilitates the development of a cross-case analysis tailored to the specific interests of its readers (see BOX 36).[2]

The fourth and last type of written product applies to multiple-case studies only. In this situation, there may be *no* separate chapters or sections devoted to the individual cases. Rather, your entire report may consist of the cross-case analysis, whether purely descriptive or also covering explanatory topics. In such a report, each chapter or section would be devoted to a separate cross-case issue, and the information from the individual cases would be dispersed throughout each chapter or section. With this format, summary information about the individual cases, if not ignored altogether (see BOX 37), might be presented in abbreviated vignettes.

As a final note, the specific type of case study composition, involving a choice among at least these four alternatives, should be identified during

---

BOX 37

A. Writing a Multiple-Case Report: An Example in Which No Single Cases Are Presented

In a multiple-case study, the individual case studies need not always be presented in the final manuscript. The individual cases, in a sense, serve only as the evidentiary base for the study and may be used solely in the cross-case analysis.

This approach was used in *The Administrative Behavior of Federal Bureau Chiefs,* a book about six federal bureau chiefs by Herbert Kaufman (1981). Kaufman spent intensive periods of time with each chief to understand his day-to-day routine. He interviewed the chiefs, listened in on their phone calls, attended meetings, and was present during staff discussions in the chiefs' offices.

The book's purpose, however, was not to portray any single one of these chiefs. Rather, the book synthesizes the lessons from all of them and is organized around such topics as how chiefs decide things, how they receive and review information, and how they motivate their staffs. Under each topic, Kaufman draws appropriate examples from the six cases, but none of the six is presented as a single-case study.

B. Writing a Multiple-Case Report: An Example (From Another Field) in Which No Single Cases Are Presented

A design similar to Kaufman's is used in another field—history—in a famous book by Crane Brinton (1938), *The Anatomy of a Revolution.* Brinton's book is based on four revolutions: the English, American, French, and Russian revolutions. The book is an analysis and theory of revolutionary periods, with pertinent examples drawn from each of the four "cases"; however, as in Kaufman's book, there is no attempt to present the single revolutions as individual case studies.

---

the *design* of the case study. Your initial choice can always be altered, as unexpected conditions may arise, and a different type of composition may become more relevant than the one originally selected. However, early selection will facilitate both the design and the conduct of the case study. Such an initial selection should be part of the case study protocol, alerting you to the likely nature of the final composition and its requirements.

CASE STUDY REPORTS AS PART OF
LARGER, MULTIMETHOD STUDIES

Your completed case study may include data from other methods (e.g., surveys or quantitative analysis of archival data such as student achievement tests). In particular, Chapter 2 pointed to the possibility that within a single case might exist embedded units of analysis, which might have been the subject of data collection through these other methods (see Chapter 2, Figure 2.4). In this situation, *the case study encompasses the other methods,* and your completed case study report would incorporate the reporting of the data from these other methods (e.g., see Chapter 4, BOX 18).

A totally different situation occurs when your case study has been deliberately designed to be part of a larger, multimethod study. In this situation, *the larger study encompasses the case study.* The larger study will contain your completed case study but also should report separately the findings about the data from the other methods. The larger study's overall report would then be based on the pattern of evidence from both the case study and the other methods. This multimethod situation deserves a bit more attention so that you will understand its implications for your case study, even though you might not compose your case study report any differently than if it had been a "stand-alone" report.

At least three different rationales might have motivated the larger study to use multiple methods. First, the larger study may have called for multiple methods simply to determine whether converging evidence (triangulation) might be obtained even though different methods had been used (Datta, 1997). In this scenario, your case study would have shared the same initial research questions as those driving the other methods, but you would likely have conducted, analyzed, and reported your case study independently. Part of the larger study's assessment would then be to compare the case study results with those based on the other methods.

Second, the larger study may have been based on a survey or quantitative analysis of archival data—for example, a study of households' financial situations under welfare reform. The larger study might then have wanted case studies to illustrate, in greater depth, the experiences of individual families. In this scenario, the questions for your case study might only have emerged *after* the survey or archival data had been analyzed, and the selection of cases might have come from the pool of those surveyed or contained within the archival records. The main implications for your case study effort are that both its timing and direction may depend on the progress and findings of the other inquiries.

Third, the larger study might knowingly have called for case studies to elucidate some underlying process and used another method (such as a

---

BOX 38

Integrating Case Study and Survey Evidence:
Complementarity of Findings

Multimethod studies can pose complementary questions that are to be addressed by different methods. Most commonly, case studies are used to gain insight into causal processes, whereas surveys provide an indication of the prevalence of a phenomenon. Two studies illustrate this combination.

The first was a study of educational projects funded by the U.S. Department of Education (Berman & McLaughlin, 1974-1978). The study combined case studies of 29 projects with a survey of 293 projects, revealing invaluable information on the implementation process and its outcomes. The second study (Yin, 1979) combined case studies of 19 sites with a survey of 90 other sites. The findings contributed to understanding the life cycle of technological innovations in local public services.

---

survey) to define the prevalence or frequency of such processes. In this scenario of complementarity as opposed to convergence, the case study questions are likely to be closely coordinated with those of the other methods, the complementary inquiries can occur simultaneously or sequentially, but the initial analysis and reports from each inquiry should be conducted independently (even though the final analysis may merge findings from all the different methods). BOX 38 contains two examples of larger studies done under this third scenario.

These three different situations show how your case study and its reporting may have to be coordinated within some broader context. Until now, this book has ignored such a context and has assumed that you have been conducting an independent case study. Beware that when your case study is not independent, you may have to coordinate deadlines and technical directions with others, and your case study report may not proceed as you might have expected initially. Also assess carefully your willingness or ability to be part of a larger team before making any commitments.

ILLUSTRATIVE STRUCTURES
FOR CASE STUDY COMPOSITIONS

The chapters, sections, subtopics, and other components of a report must be organized in some way, and this constitutes your case study report's compositional structure. Attending to such structure has been a topic of

Type of Structure	Purpose of Case Study (single- or multiple-case)		
	Explanatory	Descriptive	Exploratory
1. Linear-analytic	✕	✕	✕
2. Comparative	✕	✕	✕
3. Chronological	✕	✕	✕
4. Theory building	✕		✕
5. "Suspense"	✕		
6. Unsequenced		✕	

Figure 6.1   Six Structures and Their Application to Different Purposes of Case Studies

attention with other methodologies. For instance, Kidder and Judd (1986, pp. 430-431) write of the "hourglass" shape of a report for quantitative studies. Similarly, in ethnography, John Van Maanen (1988) has developed the concept of "tales" for reporting fieldwork results. He identifies several different types of tales: realist tales, confessional tales, impressionist tales, critical tales, formal tales, literary tales, and jointly told tales. These different types may be used in different combinations in the same report.

Alternatives also exist for structuring case study reports. This section suggests six illustrative structures (see Figure 6.1), which may be used with any of the types of case study formats just described. The illustrations are described mainly in relation to the composition of a single-case study, although the principles are readily translatable into multiple-case reports. As a further note and as indicated in Figure 6.1, the first three are all applicable to descriptive, exploratory, and explanatory case studies. The fourth is applicable mainly to exploratory and explanatory case studies, the fifth to explanatory cases, and the sixth to descriptive cases.

Linear-Analytic Structures

This is a standard approach for composing research reports. The sequence of subtopics starts with the issue or problem being studied and a review of the relevant prior literature. The subtopics then proceed to cover the methods used, the findings from the data collected and analyzed, and the conclusions and implications from the findings.

Most journal articles in experimental science reflect this type of structure, as do many case studies. The structure is comfortable to most investigators and probably is the most advantageous when research colleagues or a thesis or dissertation committee comprises the main audience for a case study. Note that the structure is applicable to explanatory, descriptive, or exploratory case studies. For example, an exploratory case may cover the issue or problem being explored, the methods of exploration, the findings from the exploration, and the conclusions (for further research).

Comparative Structures

A comparative structure repeats the same case study two or more times, comparing alternative descriptions or explanations of the same case. This is best exemplified in Allison and Zelikow's (1999) noted case study on the Cuban missile crisis (see Chapter 1, BOX 1). In this book, the authors repeat the "facts" of the case study three times, each time in conjunction with a different conceptual model. The purpose of the repetition is to show the degree to which the facts fit each model, and the repetitions actually illustrate a pattern-matching technique at work.

A similar approach can be used even if a case study is serving descriptive, and not explanatory, purposes. The same case can be described repeatedly, from different points of view or with different descriptive models, to determine how the case might best be categorized for descriptive purposes—as in arriving at the correct diagnosis for a clinical patient in psychology. Of course, other variants of the comparative approach are possible, but the main feature is that the entire case study (or the results of the cross-case analysis) is repeated two or more times in an overtly comparative mode.

Chronological Structures

Because case studies generally cover events over time, a third type of approach is to present the case study evidence in chronological order. Here, the sequence of chapters or sections might follow the early, middle, and late phases of a case history. This approach can serve an important purpose in doing explanatory case studies because presumed causal sequences must occur linearly over time. If a presumed cause of an event occurs after the event has occurred, one would have reason to question the initial causal proposition.

Whether for explanatory or descriptive purposes, a chronological approach has one pitfall to be avoided: Disproportionate attention is usually given to the early events and insufficient attention to the later ones. Most commonly, an investigator will expend too much effort in composing the introduction to a case, including its early history and background, and leave insufficient time to write about the current status of the case. To avoid this situation, one recommendation, when using a chronological structure, is to *draft* the case study *backward.* Those chapters or sections that are about the current status of the case should be drafted first, and only after these drafts have been completed should the background to the case study be drafted. Once all drafts have been completed, you can then return to the normal chronological sequence in composing the final version of the case.

Theory-Building Structures

In this approach, the sequence of chapters or sections will follow some theory-building logic. The logic will depend on the specific topic and theory, but each chapter or section should reveal a new part of the theoretical argument being made. If structured well, the entire sequence produces a compelling statement that can be most impressive.

The approach is relevant to both explanatory and exploratory case studies, both of which can be concerned with theory building. Explanatory cases will be examining the various facets of a causal argument; exploratory cases will be debating the value of further investigating various hypotheses or propositions.

Suspense Structures

This structure inverts the linear-analytic structure described previously. The direct "answer" or outcome of a case study is, paradoxically, presented in the initial chapter or section. The remainder of the case study—and its most suspenseful parts—are then devoted to the development of an explanation of this outcome, with alternative explanations considered in the ensuing chapters or sections.

This type of approach is relevant mainly to explanatory case studies, as a descriptive case study has no especially important outcome. When used well, the suspense approach is often an engaging compositional structure.

Unsequenced Structures

An unsequenced structure is one in which the sequence of sections or chapters assumes no particular importance. This structure is often sufficient for descriptive case studies, as in the example of *Middletown* (Lynd & Lynd, 1929), cited in Chapter 5. Basically, one could change the order of the chapters in that book and not alter its descriptive value.

Descriptive case studies of organizations often exhibit the same characteristic. Such case studies cover an organization's genesis and history, its ownership and employees, its product lines, its formal lines of organization, and its financial status in separate chapters or sections. The particular order in which these chapters or sections are presented is not critical and may therefore be regarded as an unsequenced approach (also see BOX 39 for another example).

If an unsequenced structure is used, the investigator does need to attend to one other problem: a test of completeness. Thus, even though the order of the chapters or sections may not matter, the overall collection does. If certain key topics are left uncovered, the description may be regarded as incomplete. An investigator must know a topic well enough—or have related models of case studies to reference—to avoid such a shortcoming. If a case study fails, without excuse, to present a complete description, the investigator can be accused of being biased—even though the case study was only descriptive.

PROCEDURES IN DOING
A CASE STUDY REPORT

Every investigator should have a well-developed set of procedures for analyzing social science data and for composing an empirical report. Numerous texts offer good advice on how you can develop your own customized procedures, including the benefits and pitfalls of using word-processing software—which will not necessarily save time (Becker, 1986, p. 160). One common warning is that writing means rewriting—a function not commonly practiced by students and therefore underestimated during the early years of research careers (Becker, 1986, pp. 43-47). The more the rewriting, especially in response to others' comments, the better the report is likely to be. In this respect, the case study report is not much different from other research reports.

However, three important procedures pertain specifically to case studies and deserve further mention. The first deals with a general tactic for starting a composition, the second covers the problem of whether to leave the case identities anonymous, and the third describes a review procedure for increasing the *construct validity* of a case study.

BOX 39

**Unsequenced Chapters, but in a
Best-Selling Book**

A best-selling book, appealing to both popular and academic audiences, was Peters and Waterman's (1982) *In Search of Excellence.* Although the book is based on more than 60 case studies of America's most successful large businesses, the text contains only the cross-case analysis, with each chapter covering an insightful set of general characteristics associated with organizational excellence. However, the particular sequence of these chapters is alterable. The book would make a significant contribution even if the chapters were in some other order.

When and How to Start Composing

The first procedure is to start composing early in the analytic process. One guide in fact admonishes that "you cannot begin writing early enough" (Wolcott, 1990, p. 20). From nearly the beginning of an investigation, certain sections of your report will always be draftable, and this drafting should proceed even before data collection and analysis have been completed.

For instance, after the literature has been reviewed and the case study has been designed, two sections of a case study report can be drafted: the bibliography and the methodological sections. The *bibliography* can always be augmented later with new citations if necessary, but by and large the major citations will have been covered in relation to the literature review. This is therefore the time to formalize the citations, to be sure that they are complete, and to construct a draft bibliography. If some citations are incomplete, the remaining details can be tracked down while the rest of the case study proceeds. This will avoid the usual practice among researchers who do the bibliography last and who therefore spend much clerical time at the very end of their research, rather than attending to the more important (and pleasurable!) tasks of writing, rewriting, and editing.

The *methodological section* also can be drafted at this stage because the major procedures for data collection and analysis should have become part of the case study design. This section may not even become a formal part of the final narrative but may be designated as an appendix. Whether part of the text or an appendix, however, the methodological section can and should be drafted at this early stage. You will remember your methodological procedures with greater precision at this juncture.

After data collection but before analysis begins, another section that can be composed covers the *descriptive data about the cases being studied.* Whereas the methodological section should have included the issues regarding the selection of the case(s), the descriptive data should cover qualitative and quantitative information about the case(s). At this stage in the research process, you still may not have finalized your ideas about the type of case study format to be used and the type of structure to be followed. However, the descriptive data are highly likely to be useful regardless of the format or structure. Furthermore, drafting the descriptive sections, even in abbreviated form, may stimulate your thinking about the overall format and structure.

If you can draft these three sections before analysis has been completed, you will have made a major advance. Furthermore, these sections can call for substantial documentation (e.g., copies of your final case study proto-col), and the best time to assemble such documentation is at this stage of the research. You also will be at an advantage if all details—citations, references, organizational titles, and spellings of people's names— have been accurately recorded during data collection and are integrated into the text at this time (Wolcott, 1990, p. 41).

If these sections are drafted properly, more attention can then be devoted to the analysis itself, as well as to the findings and conclusions. To begin composing early also serves another important psychological function: You may get accustomed to the compositional process and have a chance to practice it before the task becomes truly awesome. Thus, if you can iden-tify other sections that can be drafted at these early stages, you should draft them as well.

Case Identities: Real or Anonymous?

Nearly every case study presents an investigator with a choice regarding the anonymity of the case. Should the case study and its informants be identified, or should the names of the entire case and its participants be disguised? Note that the anonymity issue can be raised at two levels: that of the entire case (or cases) and that of an individual person within a case (or cases).

The most desirable option is to disclose the identities of both the case and the individuals. Disclosure produces two helpful outcomes. First, the reader is able to recall any other previous information he or she may have learned about the same case—from previous research or other sources—in reading and interpreting the case report. This ability to integrate a new case study with prior research is invaluable, similar to the ability to recollect previous experimental results when reading about a new set of experiments. Second, the entire case can be reviewed more readily, so that footnotes and citations can be checked, if necessary, and appropriate criticisms can be raised about the published case.

Nevertheless, there are some occasions when anonymity is necessary. The most common rationale is that when the case study has been on a controversial topic, anonymity serves to protect the real case and its real participants. A second reason is that the issuance of the final case report may affect the subsequent actions of those that were studied. This rationale was used in Whyte's (1943/1955) famous case study, *Street Corner Society* (which was about an anonymous neighborhood, "Cornerville").[3] As a third illustrative situation, the purpose of the case study may be to portray an "ideal type," and there may be no reason for disclosing true identities in such a case. This rationale was used by the Lynds in their study *Middletown,* in which the names of the small town, its residents, and its industries all were disguised (Lynd & Lynd, 1929).

On such occasions when anonymity may appear justifiable, however, other compromises should still be sought. First, you should determine whether the anonymity of the individuals alone might be sufficient, thereby leaving the case itself to be identified accurately.

A second compromise would be to name the individuals but to avoid attributing any particular point of view or comment to a single individual, again allowing the case itself to be identified accurately. This second alternative is most relevant when you want to protect the confidentiality of specific individuals. However, the lack of attribution may not be always completely protective—you also may have to disguise the comments so that no one involved in the case can infer the likely source.

For multiple-case studies, a third compromise would be to avoid composing any single-case reports and to compose only a cross-case analysis. This last situation would be roughly parallel to the procedure used in surveys, in which the individual responses are not disclosed and in which the published report is limited to the aggregate evidence.

Only if these compromises are impossible should an investigator consider making the entire case study and its informants anonymous. However, anonymity is not to be considered a desirable choice. Not only does it eliminate some important background information about the case, but it also makes the mechanics of composing the case difficult. The case and its components must be systematically converted from their real identities to fictitious ones, and you must undergo considerable effort to keep track of the conversions. The cost of undertaking such a procedure should not be underestimated.

The Review of the Draft Case Study:
A Validating Procedure

A third procedure to be followed in doing the case study report is related to the overall quality of the study. The procedure is to have the draft report reviewed, not just by peers (as would be done for any research manuscript) but also by the participants and informants in the case. If the comments are exceptionally helpful, the investigator may even want to publish them as part of the entire case study (see BOX 40).

Such review is more than a matter of professional courtesy. The procedure has been correctly identified—but only rarely—as a way of corroborating the essential facts and evidence presented in the case report (Schatzman & Strauss, 1973, p. 134). The informants and participants may still disagree with an investigator's conclusions and interpretations, but these reviewers should not disagree over the actual facts of the case. If such disagreement emerges during the review process, an investigator knows that the case study report is not finished and that such disagreements must be settled through a search for further evidence. Often, the opportunity to review the draft also produces further evidence, as the informants and participants may remember new materials that they had forgotten during the initial data collection period.

This type of review should be followed even if the case study or some of its components are to remain anonymous. Under this condition, some recognizable version of the draft must be shared with the case study informants or participants. After they have reviewed this draft, and after any differences in facts have been settled, the investigator can disguise the identities so that only the informants or participants will know the true identities. When Whyte (1943/1955) first completed *Street Corner Society*, he followed this procedure by sharing drafts of his book with "Doc," his major informant. He notes,

> As I wrote, I showed the various parts to Doc and went over them with him in detail. His criticisms were invaluable in my revision. (p. 341)

From a methodological viewpoint, the corrections made through this process will enhance the accuracy of the case study, hence increasing the *construct validity* of the study. The likelihood of falsely reporting an event should be reduced. In addition, where no objective truth may exist—as when different participants indeed have different renditions of the same event—the procedure should help to identify the various perspectives, which can then be represented in the case study report. At the same time,

---

BOX 40

Reviewing Case Studies—and Printing the Comments

A major way of improving the quality of case studies and ensuring their construct validity is to have the draft cases reviewed by those who have been the subjects of study. This procedure was followed to an exemplary degree in a set of five case studies by Marvin Alkin et al. (1979).

Each case study was about a school district and the way that the district used evaluative information about its students' performance. As part of the analytic and reporting procedure, the draft for each case was reviewed by the informants from the relevant district. The comments were obtained in part as a result of an open-ended questionnaire devised by the investigators for just this purpose. In some instances, the responses were so insightful and helpful that the investigators not only modified their original material but also printed the responses as part of their book.

With such presentation of supplementary evidence and comments, any reader can reach his or her own conclusions about the adequacy of the cases—an opportunity that has occurred, unfortunately, all too seldom in traditional case study research.

---

you need not respond to all the comments made about the draft. For example, you are entitled to your interpretations of the evidence and should not automatically incorporate your informants' reinterpretations.

The review of the draft case study by its informants will clearly extend the period of time needed to complete the case study report. Informants, unlike academic reviewers, may use the review cycles as an opportunity to begin a fresh dialogue about various facets of the case, thereby extending the review period. You must anticipate these delays and not use them as an excuse to avoid the review process altogether. When the process has been given careful attention, the potential result is the production of a high-quality case study (see BOX 41).

WHAT MAKES AN
EXEMPLARY CASE STUDY?

In all of case study research, one of the most challenging tasks is to define an exemplary case study. Although no direct evidence is available, some speculations seem an appropriate way of concluding this book.[4]

BOX 41

Formal Reviews of Case Studies

As with any other research product, the review process plays an important role in enhancing and ensuring the quality of the final results. For case studies, such a review process should involve, at a minimum, a review of the draft case study.

One set of case studies that followed this procedure, to an exemplary degree, was sponsored by the U.S. Office of Technology Assessment (1980-1981). Each of 17 case studies, which were about medical technologies, was "seen by at least 20, and some by 40 or more, outside reviewers." Furthermore, the reviewers reflected different perspectives, including those of government agencies, professional societies, consumer and public interest groups, medical practice, academic medicine, and economics and decision sciences.

In one of the case studies, a contrary view of the case—put forth by one of the reviewers—was included as part of the final published version of the case, as well as a response by the case study authors. This type of open printed interchange adds to the reader's ability to interpret the case study's conclusions and therefore to the overall quality of the case study evidence.

The exemplary case study goes beyond the methodological procedures already highlighted throughout this book. Even if you, as a case study investigator, have followed most of the basic techniques—using a case study protocol, maintaining a chain of evidence, establishing a case study database, and so on—you still may not have produced an *exemplary* case study. The mastering of these techniques makes you a good technician but not necessarily an esteemed scientist. To take but one analogy, consider the difference between a chronicler and a historian: The former is technically correct but does not produce the insights into human or social processes provided by the latter.

Five general characteristics of an exemplary case study are described below; they are intended to help your case study to be a lasting contribution to research.

The Case Study Must Be Significant

The first general characteristic may be beyond the control of many investigators. If an investigator has access to only a few "sites," or if resources are extremely limited, the ensuing case study may have to be on a topic of only marginal significance. This situation is not likely to produce an exemplary case study. However, where choice exists, the exemplary case study is likely to be one in which

- the individual case or cases are unusual and of general public interest;
- the underlying issues are nationally important, either in theoretical terms or in policy or practical terms; or
- both of the preceding conditions have been met.

For instance, a single-case study may have been chosen because it was a revelatory case—that is, one reflecting some real-life situation that social scientists had not been able to study in the past. This revelatory case is in itself likely to be regarded as a discovery and to provide an opportunity for doing an exemplary case study. Alternatively, a critical case may have been chosen because of the desire to compare two rival propositions; if the propositions are at the core of a well-known theory—or reflect major differences in public beliefs—the case study is likely to be significant. Finally, imagine the situation in which both discovery and theory development are found within the same case study, as in a multiple-case study in which each individual case reveals a discovery but the replication across cases also adds up to a significant theoretical breakthrough. This situation truly lends itself to the production of an exemplary case study.

In contrast to these promising situations, many students select nondistinctive cases or stale theoretical issues as the topics for their case studies. This situation can be avoided, in part, by doing better homework with regard to the existing body of research. Prior to selecting a case study, the student should describe, in detail, the contribution to be made, assuming that the intended case study were to be completed successfully. If no satisfactory answer is forthcoming, the student might reconsider doing the case study.

The Case Study Must Be "Complete"

This characteristic is extremely difficult to describe operationally. However, a sense of completeness is as important in doing a case study as it is in defining a complete set of laboratory experiments (or in completing a symphony or drawing a mural). All have the problem of defining the boundaries of the effort, but few guidelines are available.

For case studies, completeness can be characterized in at least three ways. First, the complete case is one in which the boundaries of the case—that is, the distinction between the phenomenon being studied and its context—are given explicit attention. If this is done only mechanically—for example, by declaring at the outset that only arbitrary time intervals or spatial boundaries will be considered—a nonexemplary case study is likely to result. The best way is to show, through either logical argument or the presentation of evidence, that as the analytic periphery is reached, the information is of decreasing relevance to the case study. Such testing of the boundaries can occur throughout the analytic and reporting steps in doing case studies.

A second way involves the collection of evidence. The complete case study should demonstrate convincingly that the investigator expended exhaustive effort in collecting the relevant evidence. The documentation of such evidence need not be placed in the text of the case, thereby dulling its content. Footnotes, appendices, and the like will do. The overall goal, nevertheless, is to convince the reader that little relevant evidence remained untouched by the investigator, given the boundaries of the case study. This does not mean that the investigator should literally collect all available evidence—an impossible task—but that the critical pieces have been given "complete" attention. Such critical pieces, for instance, would be those representing rival propositions.

A third way concerns the absence of certain artifactual conditions. A case study is not likely to be complete if the study ended only because resources were exhausted, because the investigator ran out of time (when the semester ended), or because he or she faced other, nonresearch constraints. When a time or resource constraint is known at the outset of a study, the responsible investigator should design a case study that can be completed within such constraints, rather than reaching and possibly exceeding his or her limits. This type of design requires much experience and some good fortune. Nevertheless, these are the conditions under which an exemplary case study is likely to be produced. Unfortunately, if in contrast a severe time or resource constraint suddenly emerges in the middle of a case study, it is unlikely that the case study will become exemplary.

The Case Study Must Consider Alternative Perspectives

For explanatory case studies, one valuable approach is the consideration of rival propositions and the analysis of the evidence in terms of such rivals (see Chapter 5). However, even in doing an exploratory or a descriptive case study, the examination of the evidence from different perspectives will increase the chances that a case study will be exemplary.

For instance, a descriptive case study that fails to account for different perspectives may raise a critical reader's suspicions. The investigator may not have collected all the relevant evidence and may have attended only to the evidence supporting a single point of view. Even if the investigator was not purposefully biased, different descriptive interpretations might not have been entertained, thereby presenting a one-sided case. To this day, this type of problem persists whenever studies of organizations appear to represent the perspectives of management and not workers, social groups appear to be insensitive to issues of gender or multiculturalism, and youth programs appear to represent adult perspectives and ignore those of youths.

To represent different perspectives adequately, an investigator must seek those alternatives that most seriously challenge the design of the case study. These perspectives may be found in alternative cultural views, different theories, variations among the people or decision makers who are part of the case study, or some similar contrasts.

Many times, if an investigator describes a case study to a critical listener, the listener will immediately offer an alternative interpretation of the facts of the case. Under such circumstances, the investigator is likely to become defensive and to argue that the original interpretation was the only relevant or correct one. In fact, the exemplary case study anticipates these "obvious" alternatives, even advocates their positions as forcefully as possible, and shows—empirically—the basis on which such alternatives can be rejected.

The Case Study Must Display Sufficient Evidence

Although Chapter 4 encouraged investigators to create a case study database, the critical pieces of evidence for a case study must still be contained within the case study report. The exemplary case study is one that judiciously and effectively presents the most relevant evidence, so that a reader can reach an independent judgment regarding the merits of the analysis.

This selectiveness does not mean that the evidence should be cited in a biased manner—for example, by including only the evidence that supports an investigator's conclusions. On the contrary, the evidence should be presented neutrally, with both supporting and challenging data. The reader should then be able to conclude, independently, whether a particular interpretation is valid. The selectiveness is relevant in limiting the report to the most critical evidence and not cluttering the presentation with supportive but secondary information. Such selectiveness takes a lot of discipline among investigators, who usually want to display their entire evidentiary base, in the (false) hope that sheer volume or weight will sway the reader. (In fact, sheer volume or weight will bore the reader.)

Another goal is to present enough evidence to gain the reader's confidence that the investigator "knows" his or her subject. In doing a field study, for instance, the evidence presented should convince the reader that the investigator has indeed been in the field, made penetrating inquiries while there, and has become steeped in the issues about the case. A parallel goal exists in multiple-case studies: The investigator should show the reader that all of the single cases have been treated fairly and that the cross-case conclusions have not been biased by undue attention to one or a few of the entire array of cases.

Finally, the display of adequate evidence should be accompanied by some indication that the investigator attended to the validity of the evidence—in maintaining a chain of evidence, for example. This does not mean that all case studies need to be burdened with methodological treatises. A few judicious footnotes will serve the purpose, some words in the preface of the case study can cover the critical validating steps, or the notes to a table or figure will help. As a negative example, a figure or table that presents evidence without citing its source is an indication of sloppy research and cautions the reader to be more critical of other aspects of the case study. This is not a situation that produces exemplary case studies.

The Case Study Must Be Composed in an Engaging Manner

One last characteristic has to do with the composition of the case study report. Regardless of the medium used (a written report, an oral presentation, or another form), the report should be engaging.

For written reports, this means a clear writing style, but one that constantly entices the reader to continue reading. A good manuscript is one that "seduces" the eye. If you read such a manuscript, your eye will not want to leave the page, and you will continue to read paragraph after paragraph, page after page, until exhaustion sets in. This type of seduction should be the goal in composing any case study report.

The production of this type of writing calls for talent and experience. The more often that someone has written for the same audience, the more likely that the communication will be effective. However, the clarity of writing also increases with rewriting, which is highly recommended. With the use of electronic writing tools, an investigator has no excuse for shortcutting the rewriting process.

Engagement, enticement, and seduction—these are unusual characteristics of case studies. To produce such a case study requires an investigator to be enthusiastic about the investigation and to want to communicate the results widely. In fact, the good investigator might even think that the case study contains earth-shattering conclusions. This sort of enthusiasm should pervade the entire investigation and will indeed lead to an exemplary case study.

EXERCISES

1. *Defining the audience.* Name the alternative audiences for a case study you might compose. For each audience, indicate the features of the case study report that you should highlight or de-emphasize. Would the same report serve all the audiences, and why?

2. *Reducing the barriers to composition.* Everyone has difficulties in composing reports, whether case studies or not. To succeed at composing, investigators must take specific steps during the conduct of a study to reduce barriers to composition. Name five such steps that you would take—such as starting on a portion of the composition at an early stage. Have you used these five steps in the past?

3. *Anticipating the difficulties of the review process.* Case study reports are likely to be improved by having some review by informants—that is, those persons who were the subjects of the study. Discuss the pros and cons of having such reviews. What specific advantage, for quality control purposes, is served? What disadvantages are there? On balance, are such reviews worthwhile?

4. *Maintaining anonymity in case studies.* Identify a case study whose "case" has been given a fictitious name (e.g., see BOXES 2, 8, 9, and 14 in this book). What are the advantages and disadvantages of using such a technique? What approach would you use in reporting your own case study, and why?

5. *Defining a good case study.* Select a case study that you believe is one of the best you know (the selection can be from the BOXES in this book). What makes it a good case study? Why are such characteristics so infrequently found in other case studies? What specific efforts might you make to emulate such a good case study?

NOTES

1. Ignored here is a frequent audience for case studies: students taking a course using case studies as curriculum materials. Such use of case studies, as indicated in Chapter 1, is for teaching and not research purposes, and the entire case study strategy might be defined and pursued differently under these conditions.

2. Chapter 2 of the companion book (Yin, 2003) contains a complete example of a case study from the report cited in BOX 36, demonstrating the question-and-answer format.

3. Of course, even when an investigator makes the identity of a case or its participants anonymous, a few other colleagues—sharing the confidence of the investigator—will usually know the real identities. In the case of both *Street Corner Society* and *Middletown,* other sociologists, especially those working in the same academic departments as Whyte and the Lynds, were quite aware of the real identities.

4. The speculations also are based on some empirical findings. As part of an earlier investigation, 21 prominent social scientists were asked to name the best qualities of case studies (see COSMOS, 1983). Some of these qualities are reflected in this discussion of exemplary case studies.

References

Agranoff, R., & Radin, B. A. (1991). The comparative case study approach in public administration. *Research in Public Administration, 1,* 203-231.

Alkin, M., et al. (1979). *Using evaluations: Does evaluation make a difference?* Beverly Hills, CA: Sage.

Allison, G. T. (1971). *Essence of decision: Explaining the Cuban missile crisis.* Boston: Little, Brown.

Allison, G. T., & Zelikow, P. (1999). *Essence of decision: Explaining the Cuban missile crisis* (2nd ed.). New York: Addison Wesley Longman.

Barzun, J., & Graff, H. (1985). *The modern researcher* (4th ed.). New York: Harcourt Brace Jovanovich.

Basu, O. N., Dirsmith, M. W., & Gupta, P. P. (1999). The coupling of the symbolic and the technical in an institutionalized context. *American Sociological Review, 64,* 506-526.

Becker, H. S. (1958). Problems of inference and proof in participant observation. *American Sociological Review, 23,* 652-660.

Becker, H. S. (1963). Becoming a marijuana user. In H. S. Becker (Ed.), *The outsiders* (pp. 41-58). New York: Free Press.

Becker, H. S. (1967). Whose side are we on? *Social Problems, 14,* 239-247.

Becker, H. S. (1986). *Writing for social scientists: How to start and finish your thesis, book, or article.* Chicago: University of Chicago Press.

Becker, H. S. (1998). *Tricks of the trade: How to think about your research while you're doing it.* Chicago: University of Chicago Press.

Berman, P., & McLaughlin, M. (1974-1978). *Federal programs supporting educational change* (8 vols.). Santa Monica, CA: RAND.

Bickman, L. (1987). The functions of program theory. In L. Bickman (Ed.), *Using program theory in evaluation* (pp. 5-18). San Francisco: Jossey-Bass.

Bickman, L., & Rog, D. J. (Eds.). (2000). *Handbook of applied research methods.* Thousand Oaks, CA: Sage.

Blalock, H. M., Jr. (1961). *Causal inferences in nonexperimental research.* New York: Norton.

Blau, P. M. (1955). *The dynamics of bureaucracy.* Chicago: University of Chicago Press.

Boruch, R. (1993). *Conducting randomized experiments.* Thousand Oaks, CA: Sage.

Boruch, R., & Foley, E. (2000). The honestly experimental society. In L. Bickman (Ed.), *Validity & social experimentation: Donald Campbell's legacy* (pp. 193-238). Thousand Oaks, CA: Sage.

Bouchard, T. J., Jr. (1976). Field research methods. In M. D. Dunnette (Ed.), *Industrial and organizational psychology* (pp. 363-413). Chicago: Rand McNally.

Boyatzis, R. E. (1998). *Transforming qualitative information: Thematic analysis and code development.* Thousand Oaks, CA: Sage.

Bradshaw, T. K. (1999). Communities not fazed: Why military base closures may not be catastrophic. *Journal of the American Planning Association, 65,* 193-206.

Brinton, C. (1938). *The anatomy of a revolution.* Englewood Cliffs, NJ: Prentice Hall.

Campbell, D. T. (1969). Reforms as experiments. *American Psychologist, 24,* 409-429.

Campbell, D. T. (1975). Degrees of freedom and the case study. *Comparative Political Studies, 8,* 178-193.

Campbell, D. T., & Stanley, J. (1966). *Experimental and quasi-experimental designs for research*. Chicago: Rand McNally.

Campbell, J. P., Daft, R. L., & Hulin, C. L. (1982). *What to study: Generating and developing research questions*. Beverly Hills, CA: Sage.

Carroll, J., & Johnson, E. (1992). Decision research: A field guide. *Journal of the Operational Research Society, 43*, 71-72.

Caulley, D. N., & Dowdy, I. (1987). Evaluation case histories as a parallel to legal case histories. *Evaluation and Program Planning, 10*, 359-372.

Chaskin, R. J. (2001). Building community capacity: A definitional framework and case studies from a comprehensive community initiative. *Urban Affairs Review, 36*, 291-323.

Cochran, W. G., & Cox, G. M. (1957). *Experimental designs* (2nd ed.). New York: John Wiley.

Cook, T. D., & Campbell, D. T. (1979). *Quasi-experimentation: Design and analysis issues for field settings*. Chicago: Rand McNally.

Cooper, H. M. (1984). *The integrative research review*. Beverly Hills, CA: Sage.

Cooper, H. M., & Hedges, L. V. (Eds.). (1994). *The handbook of research synthesis*. New York: Russell Sage Foundation.

COSMOS Corporation. (1983). *Case studies and organizational innovation: Strengthening the connection*. Bethesda, MD: Author.

COSMOS Corporation. (1984a). *Microcomputer implementation in schools*. Bethesda, MD: Author.

COSMOS Corporation. (1984b). *The utilization of research: Lessons from a multi-disciplined field*. Bethesda, MD: Author.

COSMOS Corporation. (1998). *Evaluation of MEP-SBDC partnerships: Final report*. Report prepared for the National Institute of Standards and Technology, U.S. Department of Commerce, Gaithersburg, MD.

COSMOS Corporation. (1999). *Evaluation of the CDC-supported technical assistance network for community planning*. Report prepared for the Centers for Disease Prevention and Control, Atlanta, GA.

COSMOS Corporation. (2000). Cross-case analysis of transformed firms. In *More transformed firms case studies* (pp. 111-123). Gaithersburg, MD: National Institute of Standards and Technology, U.S. Department of Commerce.

COSMOS Corporation. (2001). *Reforming K-12 mathematics and science education: Ongoing lessons*. Report prepared for the National Science Foundation, Arlington, VA.

Crabtree, B. F., & Miller, W. L. (Eds.). (1999). *Doing qualitative research* (2nd ed.). Thousand Oaks, CA: Sage.

Crane, J. (Ed.). (1998). *Social programs that work*. New York: Russell Sage Foundation.

Creswell, J. W. (1998). *Qualitative inquiry and research design: Choosing among five traditions*. Thousand Oaks, CA: Sage.

Crewe, K. (2001). The quality of participatory design: The effects of citizen input on the design of the Boston Southwest Corridor. *APA Journal, 67*, 437-455.

Cronbach, L. J., et al. (1980). *Toward reform of program evaluation: Aims, methods, and institutional arrangements*. San Francisco: Jossey-Bass.

Dabbs, J. M., Jr. (1982). Making things visible. In J. Van Maanen et al. (Eds.), *Varieties of qualitative research* (pp. 31-63). Beverly Hills, CA: Sage.

Datta, L. (1997). Multimethod evaluations. In E. Chelimsky & W. R. Shadish (Eds.), *Evaluation for the 21st century* (pp. 344-359). Thousand Oaks, CA: Sage.

Denzin, N. K. (1978). The logic of naturalistic inquiry. In N. K. Denzin (Ed.), *Sociological methods: A sourcebook*. New York: McGraw-Hill.

Denzin, N. K., & Lincoln, Y. S. (Eds.). (1994). *Handbook of qualitative research*. Thousand Oaks, CA: Sage.

Derthick, M. (1972). *New towns in-town: Why a federal program failed*. Washington, DC: The Urban Institute.

Drucker, P. F. (1986). The changed world economy. In P. F. Drucker (Ed.), *The frontiers of management* (pp. 21-49). New York: Dutton.

Eckstein, H. (1975). Case study and theory in political science. In F. I. Greenstein & N. W. Polsby (Eds.), *Strategies of inquiry* (pp. 79-137). Reading, MA: Addison-Wesley.

Eisenhardt, K. M. (1989). Building theories from case study research. *Academy of Management Review, 14*(4), 532-550.

Elmore, R. F., Abelmann, C. H., & Fuhrman, S. H. (1997). The new accountability in state education reform: From process to performance. In H. F. Ladd (Ed.), *Holding schools accountable* (pp. 65-98). Washington, DC: Brookings Institution.

Feagin, J. R., Orum, A. M., & Sjoberg, G. (Eds.). (1991). *A case for the case study*. Chapel Hill: University of North Carolina Press.

Fetterman, D. (1989). *Ethnography: Step by step*. Newbury Park, CA: Sage.

Fiedler, J. (1978). *Field research: A manual for logistics and management of scientific studies in natural settings*. San Francisco: Jossey-Bass.

Fielding, N. G., & Lee, R. M. (1998). *Computer analysis and qualitative research*. Thousand Oaks, CA: Sage.

Flippen, C. (2001). Neighborhood transition and social organization: The White to Hispanic case. *Social Problems, 48,* 299-321.

Fowler, F. J., Jr. (1988). *Survey research methods* (Rev. ed.). Newbury Park, CA: Sage.

Friesema, P., et al. (1979). *Aftermath: Communities after natural disasters*. Beverly Hills, CA: Sage.

Gahan, C., & Hannibal, M. (1999). *Doing qualitative research using QSR NUD·IST*. Thousand Oaks, CA: Sage.

Gans, H. J. (1962). *The urban villagers: Group and class in the life of Italian-Americans*. New York: Free Press.

George, A. L. (1979). Case studies and theory development: The method of structured, focused comparison. In P. G. Lauren (Ed.), *Diplomacy: New approaches in history, theory, and policy* (pp. 43-68). New York: Free Press.

Ghauri, P., & Grønhaug, K. (2002). *Research methods in business studies: A practical guide*. Harlow, England: Pearson Education.

Gilgun, J. F. (1994). A case for case studies in social work research. *Social Work, 39,* 371-380.

Glaser, B., & Strauss, A. (1967). *The discovery of grounded theory: Strategies for qualitative research*. Chicago: Aldine.

Gottschalk, L. (1968). *Understanding history: A primer of historical method*. New York: Knopf.

Gross, N., et al. (1971). *Implementing organizational innovations*. New York: Basic Books.

Guba, E. G., & Lincoln, Y. S. (1981). *Effective evaluation*. San Francisco: Jossey-Bass.

Guba, E. G., & Lincoln, Y. S. (1989). *Fourth generation evaluation*. Newbury Park, CA: Sage.

Hamel, J. (Ed.). (1992, Spring). The case study method in sociology [Whole issue]. *Current Sociology, 40.*

Hammond, P. E. (1968). *Sociologists at work: Essays on the craft of social research*. Garden City, NY: Doubleday.

Hanna, K. S. (2000). The paradox of participation and the hidden role of information. *Journal of the American Planning Association, 66,* 398-410.

Hedrick, T., Bickman, L., & Rog, D. J. (1993). *Applied research design*. Newbury Park, CA: Sage.

Herriott, R. E., & Firestone, W. A. (1983). Multisite qualitative policy research: Optimizing description and generalizability. *Educational Researcher, 12,* 14-19.

Hersen, M., & Barlow, D. H. (1976). *Single-case experimental designs: Strategies for studying behavior.* New York: Pergamon.

Hoaglin, D. C., Light, R. J., McPeek, B., Mosteller, F., & Stoto, M. A. (1982). *Data for decisions: Information strategies for policymakers.* Cambridge, MA: Abt Books.

Hooks, G. (1990). The rise of the Pentagon and U.S. state building: The defense program as industrial policy. *American Journal of Sociology, 96,* 358-404.

Jacob, E. (1987). Qualitative research traditions: A review. *Review of Educational Research, 57,* 1-50.

Jacob, E. (1989). Qualitative research: A defense of traditions. *Review of Educational Research, 59,* 229-235.

Jacobs, G. (Ed.). (1970). *The participant observer: Encounters with social reality.* New York: Braziller.

Jacobs, J. (1961). *The death and life of great American cities.* New York: Random House.

Jacobs, R. N. (1996). Civil society and crisis: Culture, discourse, and the Rodney King beating. *American Journal of Sociology, 101,* 1238-1272.

Jorgensen, D. (1989). *Participant observation: A methodology for human studies.* Newbury Park, CA: Sage.

Kaufman, H. (1981). *The administrative behavior of federal bureau chiefs.* Washington, DC: Brookings Institution.

Keating, W. D., & Krumholz, N. (Eds.). (1999). *Rebuilding urban neighborhoods: Achievements, opportunities, and limits.* Thousand Oaks, CA: Sage.

Kelling, G. L., & Coles, C. M. (1997). *Fixing broken windows: Restoring order and reducing crime in our communities.* New York: Simon & Schuster.

Kennedy, M. M. (1976). Generalizing from single case studies. *Evaluation Quarterly, 3,* 661-678.

Kidder, L. (1981). Qualitative research and quasi-experimental frameworks. In M. Brewer et al. (Eds.), *Scientific inquiry and the social sciences* (pp. 227-256). San Francisco: Jossey-Bass.

Kidder, L., & Judd, C. M. (1986). *Research methods in social relations* (5th ed.). New York: Holt, Rinehart & Winston.

Kidder, T. (1981). *The soul of a new machine.* Boston: Little, Brown.

Kratochwill, T. R. (1978). *Single subject research.* New York: Academic Press.

Larsen, J. (1982). *Use of knowledge in mental health services.* Palo Alto, CA: American Institutes for Research.

Latané, B., & Darley, J. M. (1969). Bystander apathy. *American Behavioral Scientist, 57,* 244-268.

Lavrakas, P. J. (1987). *Telephone survey methods.* Newbury Park, CA: Sage.

Liebow, E. (1967). *Tally's corner.* Boston: Little, Brown.

Lijphart, A. (1975). The comparable-cases strategy in comparative research. *Comparative Political Studies, 8,* 158-177.

Lincoln, Y. S. (1991). The arts and sciences of program evaluation. *Evaluation Practice, 12,* 1-7.

Lincoln, Y. S., & Guba, E. G. (1985). But is it rigorous? Trustworthiness and authenticity in naturalistic evaluation. In D. D. Williams (Ed.), *Naturalistic evaluation.* San Francisco: Jossey-Bass.

Lincoln, Y. S., & Guba, E. G. (1986). *Naturalistic inquiry.* Newbury Park, CA: Sage.

Lipset, S. M., Trow, M., & Coleman, J. (1956). *Union democracy: The inside politics of the International Typographical Union.* New York: Free Press.

Lipsey, M. W. (1992). Meta-analysis in evaluation research: Moving from description to explanation. In H. T. Chen & P. Rossi (Eds.), *Using theory to improve program and policy evaluations* (pp. 229-241). New York: Greenwood.

Llewellyn, K. N. (1948). Case method. In E. Seligman & A. Johnson (Eds.), *Encyclopedia of the social sciences.* New York: Macmillan.

Lynd, R. S., & Lynd, H. M. (1929). *Middletown: A study in modern American culture.* New York: Harcourt Brace Jovanovich.

Magaziner, I. C., & Patinkin, M. (1989). *The silent war: Inside the global business battles shaping America's future.* New York: Random House.

Markus, M. L. (1983). Power, politics, and MIS implementation. *Communications of the ACM, 26,* 430-444.

Marshall, C., & Rossman, G. B. (1989). *Designing qualitative research.* Newbury Park, CA: Sage.

McAdams, D. R. (2000). *Fighting to save our urban schools . . . and winning! Lessons from Houston.* New York: Teachers College Press.

McClintock, C. (1985). Process sampling: A method for case study research on administrative behavior. *Educational Administration Quarterly, 21,* 205-222.

Merton, R. K., Fiske, M., & Kendall, P. L. (1990). *The focused interview: A manual of problems and procedures* (2nd ed.). New York: Free Press.

Miles, M. B., & Huberman, A. M. (1994). *Qualitative data analysis: An expanded sourcebook.* Thousand Oaks, CA: Sage.

Moore, B., Jr. (1966). *Social origins of dictatorship and democracy: Lord and peasant in the making of the modern world.* Boston: Beacon.

Morris, L. L., Fitz-Gibbon, C. T., & Freeman, M. E. (1987). *How to communicate evaluation findings.* Beverly Hills, CA: Sage.

Mosteller, F., & Wallace, D. L. (1984). *Applied Bayesian and classical inference: The case of "The Federalist" papers* (2nd ed.). New York: Springer Verlag.

Murphy, J. T. (1980). *Getting the facts: A fieldwork guide for evaluators and policy analysts.* Santa Monica, CA: Goodyear.

Nachmias, D., & Nachmias, C. (1992). *Research methods in the social sciences.* New York: St. Martin's.

Naumes, W., & Naumes, M. J. (1999). *The art & craft of case writing.* Thousand Oaks, CA: Sage.

Neuman, S. B., & Celano, D. (2001). Access to print in low-income and middle-income communities: An ecological study of four neighborhoods. *Reading Research Quarterly, 36,* 8-26.

Neustadt, R. E., & Fineberg, H. (1983). *The epidemic that never was: Policy-making and the swine flu affair.* New York: Vintage.

Patton, M. Q. (1987). *How to use qualitative methods in evaluation.* Newbury Park, CA: Sage.

Patton, M. Q. (1990). *Qualitative evaluation and research methods* (2nd ed.). Thousand Oaks, CA: Sage.

Pelz, D. C. (1981). *Use of innovation in innovating processes by local governments.* Ann Arbor: University of Michigan, CRUSK, Institute for Social Research.

Perry, J. M., & Kraemer, K. L. (1986). Research methodology in the public administration review. *Public Administration Review, 46,* 215-226.

Peters, T. J., & Waterman, R. H., Jr. (1982). *In search of excellence.* New York: Harper & Row.

Peterson, K. A., & Bickman, L. (1992). Using program theory in quality assessments of children's mental health services. In H. T. Chen & P. Rossi (Eds.), *Using theory to improve program and policy evaluations* (pp. 165-176). New York: Greenwood.

Philliber, S. G., Schwab, M. R., & Samsloss, G. (1980). *Social research: Guides to a decision-making process.* Itasca, IL: Peacock.

Platt, J. (1992a). "Case study" in American methodological thought. *Current Sociology, 40,* 17-48.

Platt, J. (1992b). Cases of cases . . . of cases. In C. C. Ragin & H. S. Becker (Eds.), *What is a case? Exploring the foundations of social inquiry* (pp. 21-52). New York: Cambridge University Press.

Pressman, J. L., & Wildavsky, A. (1973). *Implementation: How great expectations in Washington are dashed in Oakland.* Berkeley: University of California Press.

Raizen, S. A., & Britton, E. D. (Eds.). (1997). *Bold ventures* (3 vols.). Dordrecht, The Netherlands: Kluwer Academic.

Redman, E. (1973). *The dance of legislation.* New York: Simon & Schuster.

Rog, D. J., & Huebner, R. B. (1992). Using research and theory in developing innovative programs for homeless individuals. In H. T. Chen & P. Rossi (Eds.), *Using theory to improve program and policy evaluations* (pp. 129-144). New York: Greenwood.

Rosenbaum, D. P. (Ed.). (1986). *Community crime prevention: Does it work?* Thousand Oaks, CA: Sage.

Rosenthal, R. (1966). *Experimenter effects in behavioral research.* New York: Appleton-Century-Crofts.

Rubin, A., & Babbie, E. (1993). *Research methods for social work.* Pacific Grove, CA: Brooks/Cole.

Rubin, H. J., & Rubin, I. S. (1995). *Qualitative interviewing: The art of hearing data.* Thousand Oaks, CA: Sage.

Schatzman, L., & Strauss, A. (1973). *Field research.* Englewood Cliffs, NJ: Prentice Hall.

Schorr, L. B. (1997). *Common purpose: Strengthening families and neighborhoods to rebuild America.* New York: Anchor.

Schramm, W. (1971, December). *Notes on case studies of instructional media projects.* Working paper for the Academy for Educational Development, Washington, DC.

Sechrest, L. (1991, October-November). *Roots: Back to our first generations.* Presidential remarks at the annual meeting of the American Evaluation Association, Chicago.

Selznick, P. (1980). *TVA and the grass roots: A study of politics and organization.* Berkeley: University of California Press. (Original work published 1949)

Shavelson, R., & Townes, L. (Eds.). (2002). *Scientific research in education.* Washington, DC: National Academy Press.

Sidowski, J. B. (Ed.). (1966). *Experimental methods and instrumentation in psychology.* New York: Holt, Rinehart & Winston.

Sieber, S. D. (1973). The integration of fieldwork and survey methods. *American Journal of Sociology, 78,* 1335-1359.

Silverman, D. (2000). *Doing qualitative research: A practical handbook.* Thousand Oaks, CA: Sage.

Smith, J. K., & Heshusius, L. (1986). Closing down the conversation: The end of the quantitative-qualitative debate among educational inquirers. *Educational Researcher, 15,* 4-12.

Smith, N. L. (1990). Cautions on the use of investigative case studies in meta-evaluation. *Evaluation and Program Planning, 13*(4), 373-378.

Spilerman, S. (1971). The causes of racial disturbances: Tests of an explanation. *American Sociological Review, 36,* 427-442.

Stake, R. E. (1983). The case study method in social inquiry. In G. F. Madaus, M. S. Scriven, & D. L. Stufflebeam (Eds.), *Evaluation models* (pp. 279-286). Boston: Kluwer-Nijhoff.

Stake, R. E. (1986). *Quieting reform: Social science and social action in an urban youth program*. Urbana: University of Illinois Press.

Stake, R. E. (1994). Case studies. In N. K. Denzin & Y. S. Lincoln (Eds.), *Handbook of qualitative research* (pp. 236-247). Thousand Oaks, CA: Sage.

Standerfer, N. R., & Rider, J. (1983). The politics of automating a planning office. *Planning, 49*, 18-21.

Stein, H. (1952). Case method and the analysis of public administration. In H. Stein (Ed.), *Public administration and policy development* (pp. xx-xxx). New York: Harcourt Brace Jovanovich.

Stoecker, R. (1991). Evaluating and rethinking the case study. *The Sociological Review, 39*, 88-112.

Strauss, A., & Corbin, J. (1998). *Basics of qualitative research: Techniques and procedures for developing grounded theory* (2nd ed.). Thousand Oaks, CA: Sage.

Sudman, S., & Bradburn, N. M. (1982). *Asking questions: A practical guide to questionnaire design*. San Francisco: Jossey-Bass.

Sutton, R. I., & Staw, B. M. (1995). What theory is *not*. *Administrative Science Quarterly, 40*, 371-384.

Szanton, P. (1981). *Not well advised*. New York: Russell Sage Foundation and The Ford Foundation.

Towl, A. R. (1969). *To study administrations by cases*. Boston: Harvard University Business School.

Trochim, W. (1989). Outcome pattern matching and program theory. *Evaluation and Program Planning, 12*, 355-366.

U.S. General Accounting Office, Program Evaluation and Methodology Division. (1990). *Case study evaluations*. Washington, DC: Government Printing Office.

U.S. National Commission on Neighborhoods. (1979). *People, building neighborhoods*. Washington, DC: Government Printing Office.

U.S. Office of Technology Assessment. (1980-1981). *The implications of cost-effectiveness analysis of medical technology: Case studies of medical technologies*. Washington, DC: Government Printing Office.

Van Maanen, J. (1988). *Tales of the field: On writing ethnography*. Chicago: University of Chicago Press.

Van Maanen, J., Dabbs, J. M., Jr., & Faulkner, R. R. (1982). *Varieties of qualitative research*. Beverly Hills, CA: Sage.

Wax, R. (1971). *Doing field work*. Chicago: University of Chicago Press.

Webb, E., Campbell, D. T., Schwartz, R. D., Sechrest, L., & Grove, J. B. (1981). *Nonreactive measures in the social sciences* (2nd ed.). Boston: Houghton Mifflin.

Wholey, J. (1979). *Evaluation: Performance and promise*. Washington, DC: The Urban Institute.

Whyte, W. F. (1955). *Street corner society: The social structure of an Italian slum*. Chicago: University of Chicago Press. (Original work published 1943)

Wilford, J. N. (1992). *The mysterious history of Columbus*. New York: Vintage.

Windsor, D., & Greanias, G. (1983). The public policy and management program for case/course development. *Public Administration Review, 26*, 370-378.

Wolcott, H. F. (1990). *Writing up qualitative research*. Newbury Park, CA: Sage.

Yin, R. K. (1970). Face recognition by brain-injured patients: A dissociable ability? *Neuropsychologia, 8*, 395-402.

Yin, R. K. (1978). Face perception: A review of experiments with infants, normal adults, and brain-injured persons. In R. Held, H. W. Leibowitz, & H.-L. Teuber (Eds.), *Handbook of sensory physiology: Vol. 8. Perception* (pp. 593-608). New York: Springer-Verlag.

Yin, R. K. (1979). *Changing urban bureaucracies: How new practices become routinized.* Lexington, MA: Lexington Books.

Yin, R. K. (1980). Creeping federalism: The federal impact on the structure and function of local government. In N. J. Glickman (Ed.), *The urban impacts of federal policies* (pp. 595-618). Baltimore: Johns Hopkins University Press.

Yin, R. K. (1981a). The case study as a serious research strategy. *Knowledge: Creation Diffusion, Utilization, 3,* 97-114.

Yin, R. K. (1981b). The case study crisis: Some answers. *Administrative Science Quarterly, 26,* 58-65.

Yin, R. K. (1981c). Life histories of innovations: How new practices become routinized. *Public Administration Review, 41,* 21-28.

Yin, R. K. (1982a). *Conserving America's neighborhoods.* New York: Plenum.

Yin, R. K. (1982b). Studying the implementation of public programs. In W. Williams et al (Eds.), *Studying implementation: Methodological and administrative issues* (pp. 36-72). Chatham, NJ: Chatham House.

Yin, R. K. (1982c). Studying phenomenon and context across sites. *American Behavioral Scientist, 26,* 84-100.

Yin, R. K. (1986). Community crime prevention: A synthesis of eleven evaluations. In D. P. Rosenbaum (Ed.), *Community crime prevention: Does it work?* (pp. 294-308). Thousand Oaks, CA: Sage.

Yin, R. K. (1994a). Discovering the future of the case study method in evaluation research. *Evaluation Practice, 15,* 283-290.

Yin, R. K. (1994b). Evaluation: A singular craft. In C. Reichardt & S. Rallis (Eds.), *New directions in program evaluation* (pp. 71-84). San Francisco: Jossey-Bass.

Yin, R. K. (1997, Winter). Case study evaluations: A decade of progress? *New Directions for Evaluation, 76,* 69-78.

Yin, R. K. (1999). Enhancing the quality of case studies in health services research. *Health Services Research, 34,* 1209-1224.

Yin, R. K. (2000). Rival explanations as an alternative to "reforms as experiments." In L. Bickman (Ed.), *Validity & social experimentation: Donald Campbell's legacy* (pp. 239-266). Thousand Oaks, CA: Sage.

Yin, R. K. (2003). *Applications of case study research* (2nd ed.). Thousand Oaks, CA: Sage.

Yin, R. K., & Oldsman, E. (1995). *Logic model for evaluating changes in manufacturing firms.* Unpublished paper prepared for the National Institute of Standards and Technology, U.S. Department of Commerce, Gaithersburg, MD.

Zigler, E., & Muenchow, S. (1992). *Head Start: The inside story of America's most successful educational experiment.* New York: Basic Books.

Index

Abelmann, C. H., 54
Alkin, M., 159
Allison, G. T., 3, 4, 40, 153
Analytic generalization, 32-33, 32 (figure)
Analytic strategies, 109
    case description, development of,
        114-115, 115 (box)
    cross-case synthesis, 134-137, 135-136
        (boxes), 136 (figure)
    explanation-building and, 120-123,
        121-122 (boxes)
    logic models, 127-134, 130-133
        (figures)
    need for, 109-110
    pattern matching and, 116-120,
        118 (box)
    quality in, 137-138, 139 (box)
    rival explanations and, 112-114, 113
        (figure)
    theoretical propositions and, 111-112
    time-series analysis, 123-127, 126 (box)
    tools/manipulations in, 110-111
    See also Reporting case studies

Becker, H. S., 90
Berman, P., 151
Bias, 10-11, 62, 95-96
Bickman, L., 31
Blau, P. M., 61
Boruch, R., 8
Brinton, C., 30, 149
Britton, E. D., 147

Campbell, D. T., 26, 124
CAQDAS (Computer Assisted Qualitative
    Data Analysis Software), 110
Case studies, viii, xi, 1
    contemporary focus of, 7-8
    definition of, 12-14
    design variations in, 14-15
    generalizability and, 10-11, 15, 16 (box)
    logic of design in, 13-14

methodology comparison, 3-9, 4
    (boxes), 5 (figure)
prejudices against, 10-11
quality, elements of, 160-165
question typology and, 5-7
research strategy of, 1-3
rigor of, 10
See also Data collection process;
    Reporting case studies; Research
    design
Case study designs, 39, 40 (figure)
    closed vs. flexible design, 55
    multiple-case design, 46-53, 49 (box),
        50 (figure)
    multiple vs. single design, 53-54,
        54 (box)
    single-case design, 39-46, 41-44 (boxes)
    See also Research design
Case study protocol, 67
    contents of, 67-70, 68-69 (figures)
    field procedures, 72-73
    project overview, 70-72, 71 (figure)
    question formulation, 73-76, 76 (figure)
    report guideline, 76-77
Chain-of-evidence, 105-106, 105 (figure)
Chaskin, R. J., 54
Coleman, J., 43
Coles, C. M., 122
Community trials, xi, 8
Computer-assisted telephone interviews
    (CATIs), xi
Construct validity, 34 (figure), 35-36
Craft rivals, 113, 113 (figure)
Crane, J., 16
Cross-case synthesis, 134-137, 135-136
    (boxes), 136 (figure)

Database development, 101-102
    case study notes, 102-103
    documents and, 103
    narratives, 103-105, 104 (box)
    tabular materials, 103

Data collection process, 57-58
  bias and, 62, 95-96
  case study protocol, 67-77
  chain-of-evidence and,
        105-106, 105 (figure)
  field procedures, 72-73
  flexibility/adaptiveness in,
        60-61, 61 (box)
  investigator skills set, 58-62
  knowledge base and, 61-62
  listening skills, 60
  multiple sources, 97-101, 98-99
        (boxes), 100 (figure)
  pilot case studies and, 78-80
  problems in, 66-67
  question asking, 59-60, 73-76
  routinized activity in, 58
  screening data, 77-78
  training seminars for, 62-67, 63 (box),
        65 (figure)
  units of analysis and, 75-76, 76 (figure)
  See also Analytic strategy; Database
        development; Evidence collection
        process
Derthick, M., 121
Descriptive case studies, 3, 4 (box), 6
Design evaluation, 33-35, 34 (figure)
  construct validity, 35-36
  external validity, 37-38, 37 (box)
  internal validity, 36
  reliability, 38-39
  See also Case study designs; Research
        design
Documentation. *See* Evidence collection
        process; Reporting case studies
Drucker, P. F., 23, 29

Elmore, R. F., 54
Embedded case study design, 43-45, 43-44
        (box), 52-53
Ethnography, 11, 14
Evaluation research, xi, 8-9, 15
Evaluative tests. *See* Design evaluation
Evidence collection process, 83
  archival records, 88-89
  chain-of-evidence, maintenance of,
        105-106, 105 (figure)
  database development,
        101-105, 104 (box)

  direct observations, 92-93, 93 (box)
  documentary information, 85-88,
        88 (boxes)
  interviews, 89-92, 91 (box)
  methodological texts, 83-84
  multiple-source principle, 97-101
  narratives, 103-105, 104 (box)
  participant-observation, 93-96,
        94-95 (boxes)
  physical artifacts, 96
  sources of evidence, 85, 86 (figure)
  triangulation and, 97-99, 98-99 (boxes),
        100 (figure)
  See also Analytic strategy; Data
        collection process
Experimental method, viii, 8, 20, 137
Explanation-building process, 120
  elements of explanations, 120, 121 (box)
  iterative nature of, 120-122, 122 (box)
  problems in, 122-123
Explanatory case studies, 3, 4 (box), 6
Exploratory case studies, 5-6, 22, 23 (box)
External validity, 34 (figure), 37-38,
        37 (box)

Feagin, J. R., 23
Field procedures, 63 (box), 72-73
Fineberg, H., 145
Foley, E., 8
Friesema, P., 126
Fuhrman, S. H., 54

Gans, H. J., 94
Generalization, 10-11, 15, 16 (box)
  external validity testing and, 37-38,
        38 (box)
  single-case testimony and, 144-145
  theory development and, 31-33,
        32 (figure)
Gross, N., 41
Group theories, 31

Hanna, K. S., 91
Hermeneutics, vii-viii
Hierarchical linear models (HLMs), xi, 3
Holistic case study design, 2, 43-45, 52-53
Hooks, G., 134
Huberman, A. M., 110
Individual theories, 31

Inference. *See* Generalization
Internal validity, 34 (figure), 36, 116
Interviews, xi, 89-90
    computer-assisted telephone
        interviews, xi
    data corroboration and, 92
    focused interviews, 90-91
    open-ended interviews, 90
    recording devices in, 92
    surveys, 91, 91 (box)
Investigative skills. *See* Data
    collection process

Jacobs, J., 37
Judd, C. M., 152

Kaufman, H., 149
Kelling, G. L., 122
Kidder, L., 123, 152
Kidder, T., 25

Liebow, E., 42
Lipset, S. N., 43
Logic models, 127-128
    alternative configuration for, 129,
        132-133, 132 (figure)
    definition/testing of, 134
    individual-level, 128-129, 130 (figure)
    organizational-level, 129, 131 (figure),
        132-133
    program-level, 133, 133 (box)
    sampling logic,48-49
Lynd, H. M., 64, 114, 155, 158
Lynd, R. S., 64, 114, 155, 158

Magaziner, I. C., 25, 138
McLaughlin, M., 151
Miles, M. B., 110
Moore, B., Jr., 121
Muenchow, S., 98
Multi-method studies, 2, 150-151, 151 (box)
Multiple-case studies, 2, 10, 45-46
    holistic vs. embedded design and, 52-53
    numerical sufficiency in, 51
    replication logic and, 47-51, 49 (box),
        50 (figure)
    sampling logic and, 48-49
    theory development and, 48
    time-series analysis and, 124

See also Analytic strategies; Case study
        design; Reporting case studies
Multiple-source evidence, 97
    convergence/non-convergence of, 99,
        100 (figure)
    prerequisites for, 99-101
    triangulation and, 97-99, 98-99 (boxes)

Narratives, 103-105, 104 (box)
Neustadt, R. E., 145
NUD-IST (non-numerical unstructured
        data indexing, searching, and
        theorizing), 110

Observational evidence, 92-93, 93 (box)
Oldsman, E., 131
Organizational theories, 31
Orum, A. M., 23

Participant-observation, 11, 12, 93-96,
        95 (boxes)
Patinkin, M., 25, 138
Pattern matching, ix, 26-27, 27 (figure), 116
    non-equivalent dependent variables,
        116-118
    precision in, 119-120
    rival explanations, 118-119, 118 (box)
    simple patterns/minimal variety, 119
    See also Time-series analysis
Patton, M. Q., 98
Peters, T. J., 155
Pilot case studies, 78-79
    nature of, 80
    reports from, 80
    selection of, 79
Platt, J., 12, 13, 22
Plausible rival hypotheses, vii, viii
Pressman, J. L., 115
Protocol. *See* Case study protocol

Questions:
    data collection and, 59-60
    formulation protocol, 73-76, 76 (figure)
    reporting format, 147-148, 148 (box)

Raizen, S. A., 147
Randomized-assignment-to-treatment
        models, viii, 8
Real-life rivals, 113-114, 113 (figure)

Record keeping. *See* Data collection
    process; Reporting case studies
Redman, E., 95
Reliability, 34 (figure), 38-39, 105
Replication, viii, 10, 33
Replication logic, 47-51, 49 (box),
    50 (figure)
Reporting case studies, 141-143
    audience targeting, 143-149,
        144 (boxes)
    case study protocol and, 76-77
    chronological structures, 153-154
    communication device of, 144-145,
        146 (box)
    comparative structures, 153
    compositional structures, 151-155,
        152 (figure)
    linear-analytic structures, 152-153
    multi-method studies and, 150-151,
        151 (box)
    pilot case studies, 80
    procedures in, 155-160
    quality, elements of, 160-165
    question-answer format, 147-148,
        148 (box)
    report orientation, 146
    review of, 159-160, 160 (box),
        161 (box)
    single/multiple-case reports, 146-147,
        147 (box), 148, 149 (box)
    suspense structures, 154
    theory-building structures, 154
    unsequenced structures, 154-155,
        156 (box)
    written format, 146-149,
        147-149 (boxes)
Research design, 19-20
    components of, 21-28
    definition of, 20-21
    generalization and, 31-33, 32 (figure)
    interpretation criteria in, 26-28
    propositions in, 22, 23 (box)
    questions in, 21-22
    theory development and, 28-33,
        30 (box)
    trial research, xi
    units of analysis and, 22-26,
        25 (boxes)
    work plan and, 21

See also Case study designs; Data
    collection process; Design
    evaluation
Rider, J., 144
Rival explanations, 112-114, 113 (figure),
    118-119, 118 (box)
Rosenbaum, D. P., 135

Sampling logic, 48-49
Schorr, L. B., 16
Selznick, P., 144
Single-case designs, 39, 45-46
    critical case and, 40, 41 (box)
    extreme/unique case and, 40-41
    holistic vs. embedded studies, 43-45,
        43-44 (box)
    longitudinal case and, 42
    representative/typical case and, 41
    revelatory case and, 42, 43 (box)
    vulnerability of, 43
    See also Analytic strategies; Case study
        design; Reporting case studies
Sjoberg, G., 23
Societal theories, 31
Standerfer, N. R., 144
Statistical generalization, 32, 32 (figure)
Structural equation modeling (SEM), xi
Surveys, xi, 10, 91, 91 (box)
Szanton, P., 49

Teaching practices, 2, 10
Theory development, 28-30, 30 (box)
    case study reporting and, 154
    generalization and, 31-33, 32 (figure)
    multiple-case studies and, 48, 50-51,
        50 (figure)
    theory types, 30-31
Time-series analysis, 123
    chronology development, 125-126
    complex time series, 124-125, 126 (box)
    conditions for, 126-127
    simple time series, 123-124
Training seminars. *See* Data
    collection process
Triangulation, 97-99, 98-99 (boxes)
Trow, M., 43

Units of analysis, 22-26, 25 (boxes),
    75-76, 76 (figure)

Validity, vii, 33-35, 34 (figure)
    construct validity, 35-36
    external validity, 37-38, 37 (box)
    internal validity, 36, 116
Van Maanen, J., 152

Waterman, R. H., Jr., 155
Wholey, J., 127, 128

Whyte, W. F., 3, 4, 42, 94,
    158, 160
Wildavsky, A., 115

Yin, R. K., 113, 131, 135, 151

Zelikow, P., 3, 4, 153
Zigler, E., 98

About the Author

Robert K. Yin serves as President and CEO of COSMOS Corporation, an applied research and social science firm located in Bethesda, Maryland, and in operation since 1980. Over the years, COSMOS has successfully completed hundreds of projects for government agencies, private foundations, and other for-profit and nonprofit organizations. At COSMOS, Dr. Yin actively leads research projects, including those using the case study method.

Dr. Yin has authored numerous peer-reviewed books and articles. Besides this book on the case study method, which has had Japanese and Portuguese translations, he also has authored *Applications of Case Study Research* (2nd edition, 2003). Dr. Yin received his B.A. (magna cum laude) from Harvard College (in history) and his Ph.D. from the Department of Brain and Cognitive Sciences, Massachusetts Institute of Technology. He is a member of the Cosmos Club in Washington, D.C. In 1998, he founded the "Robert K. Yin Fund" at MIT, which supports seminars on brain sciences, as well as other activities related to the advancement of pre-doctoral students at the Department of Brain and Cognitive Sciences.

APPLIED SOCIAL RESEARCH
METHODS SERIES

Series Editors
LEONARD BICKMAN, Peabody College, Vanderbilt University, Nashville
DEBRA J. ROG, Vanderbilt University, Washington, DC

32. **APPLIED RESEARCH DESIGN**
   by TERRY E. HEDRICK,
   LEONARD BICKMAN, and DEBRA J. ROG
33. **DOING URBAN RESEARCH**
   by GREGORY D. ANDRANOVICH
   and GERRY RIPOSA
34. **APPLICATIONS OF CASE STUDY
   RESEARCH
   (Second Edition)**
   by ROBERT K. YIN
35. **INTRODUCTION TO FACET THEORY**
   by SAMUEL SHYE and DOV ELIZUR
   with MICHAEL HOFFMAN
36. **GRAPHING DATA**
   by GARY T. HENRY
37. **RESEARCH METHODS IN SPECIAL
   EDUCATION**
   by DONNA M. MERTENS
   and JOHN A. McLAUGHLIN
38. **IMPROVING SURVEY QUESTIONS**
   by FLOYD J. FOWLER, Jr.
39. **DATA COLLECTION AND MANAGEMENT**
   by MAGDA STOUTHAMER-LOEBER
   and WELMOET BOK VAN KAMMEN
40. **MAIL SURVEYS**
   by THOMAS W. MANGIONE
41. **QUALITATIVE RESEARCH DESIGN**
   by JOSEPH A. MAXWELL

42. **ANALYZING COSTS, PROCEDURES,
   PROCESSES, AND OUTCOMES IN
   HUMAN SERVICES**
   by BRIAN T. YATES
43. **DOING LEGAL RESEARCH**
   by ROBERT A. MORRIS, BRUCE D. SALES,
   and DANIEL W. SHUMAN
44. **RANDOMIZED EXPERIMENTS FOR
   PLANNING AND EVALUATION**
   by ROBERT F. BORUCH
45. **MEASURING COMMUNITY
   INDICATORS**
   by PAUL J. GRUENEWALD,
   ANDREW J, TREND, GAIL TAFF,
   and MICHAEL KLITZNER
46. **MIXED METHODOLOGY**
   by ABBAS TASHAKKORI and
   CHARLES TEDDLIE
47. **NARRATIVE RESEARCH**
   by AMIA LIEBLICH, RIVKA TUVAL-
   MASHIACH, and TAMAR ZILBER
48. **COMMUNICATING SOCIAL SCIENCE
   RESEARCH TO POLICY-MAKERS**
   bY ROGER VAUGHAN and TERRY
   F. BUSS
49. **PRACTICAL META-ANALYSIS**
   by MARK W. LIPSEY and
   DAVID B. WILSON

Other volumes in this series are listed on the series page